KT-564-166

Mama's
Italian
Cookbook

Just like Mama used to make

This edition published in 2011
LOVE FOOD is an imprint of Parragon Books Ltd

Parragon
Queen Street House
4 Queen Street
Bath BA1 1HE, UK

Copyright © Parragon Books Ltd 2009

LOVE FOOD and the accompanying heart device is a registered trade mark of Parragon Books Ltd in Australia, the UK, USA, India and the EU.

All rights reserved. No part of this publication may be reproduced, stored in a retrieval system, or transmitted, in any form or by any means, electronic, mechanical, photocopying, recording, or otherwise, without the prior permission of the copyright holder.

ISBN: 978-1-4075-7700-5

Printed in China

Internal design by Sabine Vonderstein
Mama's world created by Dominic Utton
Project managed by Faye Lloyd

Mama and all characters mentioned in this book are entirely fictitious. Any similarity to any person, living or dead, is purely co-incidental and unintended.

Notes for the Reader
This book uses both metric and imperial measurements. Follow the same units of measurement throughout; do not mix metric and imperial. All spoon measurements are level: teaspoons are assumed to be 5 ml, and tablespoons are assumed to be 15 ml. Unless otherwise stated, milk is assumed to be full fat, eggs and individual vegetables are medium, and pepper is freshly ground black pepper.

The times given are an approximate guide only. Preparation times differ according to the techniques used by different people and the cooking times may also vary from those given. Optional ingredients, variations or serving suggestions have not been included in the calculations.

Recipes using raw or very lightly cooked eggs should be avoided by infants, the elderly, pregnant women, convalescents and anyone suffering from an illness. Pregnant and breastfeeding women are advised to avoid eating peanuts and peanut products. Sufferers from nut allergies should be aware that some of the ready-made ingredients used in the recipes in this book may contain nuts. Always check the packaging before use.

Contents

Introduction   8

Mama's Simple Suppers   12

Mama's Celebrations   52

Mama's Comfort Food   92

Mama's Day Out!   134

Mama's Baking Day   176

Acknowledgements   218

Index   220

Introduction

Welcome to Mama's Italian Cookbook — not only a collection of recipes from my own kitchen, but a scrapbook of family wisdom and a little insight into my life. For me, there is no distinction between the cooking and the cook: the feelings, the passion, the love and the experiences of the person making the food all go into the food… and so the cook becomes a part of the recipe. All of which means: to understand my food is to understand me.

So let me tell you about myself. People call me Mama. I'm the head of a large, noisy, happy household here in a small village in Apulia, a region in the south of Italy. I've been married to Alberto for 56 years and together we have six children, 22 grandchildren and eight great-grandchildren. I've lived in this village all of my life — and my mama, her mama and her mama before her, all did the same. Tradition is everything here.

And nowhere is tradition more clearly seen than in the kitchen. Learning how to feed a family is a skill and a passion that is passed down the generations; and it is a source of pride with me that, even in the hardest times, I have always put beautiful, healthy food on my table — and my family have grown strong and beautiful themselves as a result.

Good food needn't be complicated: simple dishes put together with care and love can be the match of the most decorated chefs in the ristoranti of Roma and Milano. In Mama's kitchen we have just one test: if four generations of the same family can sit down and enjoy a meal together, if every plate is wiped clean and every stomach satisfied, then Mama's done her job well.

Of course, I may be the head of a family over 36 strong (and I don't include myself or Alberto in that, nor our many cousins, nephews, nieces… all of whom can often be found sitting at our table or harassing

Mama in the kitchen), but naturally I'm not cooking for all of them every day. Our children have families of their own now, as do some of their children, and although our eldest boys, Marco and Filippo, now work the same olive groves that Alberto used to tend, and our youngest two, Maria and Lucia, married men from the same village and live within earshot on a clear day, our other two boys, Gianluca and Alessandro, wear suits and work in the city now. When they come home there's always a celebration, but sadly, it's not so often as any of us would like.

In the meantime, village life means there's always some work to be done in the kitchen. There's our annual fiesta, of course, and then the competitions with our neighbouring villages: and if Mama isn't competing herself (for three years running my risotti were the pride of the whole region) then I'm inevitably cooking up a victory feast of one kind or another. Add to that all the weddings, christenings, birthdays and other celebrations, and it's a wonder I ever get time to feed Alberto and the children at all!

GENOVA - Piazza della Nunziata

All of my experience has gone into this book — and all the experience of those who taught me: my mama, and her mama before her. It is not simply a collection of recipes, it's an expression of who I am.

Most cookbooks are written like textbooks — reading them is like listening to cookery teachers. This one's different. This is Mama's cookbook. And we have a saying in Apulia: 'Una buona mamma vale cento maestre' — a good mother is worth a hundred teachers.

Buon appetito!

Mama's Simple Suppers

All good cooking starts with simplicity. Get the basics — the principi fondamentali — right and all else will follow. Before you can tackle the big parties and the showcase dishes, you have to learn how to make simple suppers. These are the recipes Mama learnt as a little girl, standing on tiptoe in the kitchen, watching her mama — and they are the staple of our household mealtimes still.

What could be more heartwarming than homemade Tuscan bean soup? What could be more wholesome than spaghetti with meatballs? And what better way to finish any meal than with Mama's chocolate and nut cake?

These are the tastes of authentic Italian cooking. Enjoy!

Minestrone
Hearty vegetable and pasta soup

serves 4

2 tbsp olive oil
2 garlic cloves, chopped
2 red onions, chopped
75 g/2¾ oz prosciutto, sliced
1 red pepper, deseeded and chopped
1 orange pepper, deseeded and
  chopped
400 g/14 oz canned chopped
  tomatoes
1 litre/1¾ pints vegetable stock
1 celery stick, topped, tailed and
  sliced
400 g/14 oz canned borlotti
  beans, drained
100 g/3½ oz shredded green leafy
  cabbage
75 g/2¾ oz frozen peas, thawed
1 tbsp chopped fresh parsley
75 g/2¾ oz dried vermicelli pasta
salt and pepper
freshly grated Parmesan cheese,
  to garnish
fresh crusty bread, to serve

Heat the oil in a large saucepan. Add the garlic, onions and prosciutto and cook over a medium heat, stirring, for 3 minutes, until slightly soft. Add the red and orange peppers and the chopped tomatoes and cook for a further 2 minutes, stirring. Stir in the stock, then add the celery, beans, cabbage, peas and parsley. Season with salt and pepper.

Bring to the boil, then reduce the heat and simmer for 30 minutes.

Add the pasta to the pan. Cook for a further 10—12 minutes, or according to the instructions on the packet. Remove from the heat and ladle into warmed bowls. Garnish with some freshly grated Parmesan cheese and serve with fresh crusty bread.

Pappa al pomodoro
Bread and tomato soup

Chop the bread into rough chunks, about 2.5 cm/1 inch square. Place a heavy-based saucepan over a medium heat. Add the stock, oil and sage and simmer until reduced by half. Add the bread and garlic, increase the heat to high and fry until all the liquid has been soaked up and the bread begins to become crispy.

Add the tomatoes and sugar, stir and simmer for 15 minutes. Add hot water to thin the soup to your preferred consistency (it should be thick). Simmer for a further minute. Taste and adjust the seasoning.

Ladle into warmed bowls, sprinkle a little Parmesan cheese on top and serve.

serves 6

300 g/10½ oz sourdough bread
125 ml/4 fl oz chicken stock
4 tbsp extra virgin olive oil
3 tbsp shredded fresh sage leaves
4 garlic cloves, peeled and
   finely chopped
800 g/1 lb 12 oz canned peeled
   plum tomatoes
1 tsp sugar
225 ml/8 fl oz hot water
salt and pepper
55 g/2 oz grated Parmesan cheese,
   to garnish

Ribollita
Tuscan bean soup

serves 6

300 g/10½ oz canned cannellini
beans, drained and rinsed
300 g/10½ oz canned borlotti
beans, drained and rinsed
600 ml/1 pint vegetable stock
115 g/4 oz dried conchigliette
or other small pasta shapes
4 tbsp olive oil
2 garlic cloves,
very finely chopped
3 tbsp chopped fresh flat-leaf
parsley
salt and pepper

Place half the cannellini beans and half the borlotti beans in a food processor with half the stock and process until smooth. Pour into a large, heavy-based saucepan and add the remaining beans. Stir in enough of the remaining stock to achieve the consistency you like, then bring to the boil. Add the pasta and return to the boil, then reduce the heat and cook for 15 minutes, or until just tender.

Meanwhile, heat 3 tablespoons of the oil in a small frying pan. Add the garlic and cook, stirring constantly, for 2—3 minutes, or until golden. Stir the garlic into the soup with the parsley.

Season to taste with salt and pepper and ladle into warmed bowls. Drizzle with the remaining olive oil and serve immediately.

Mama's tips for running a smooth household

Organization is the key to an easy life: in the kitchen and out of it. Alberto knew every leaf on every branch in the olive groves — and I could cook blindfolded here if I had to. Keep your kitchen tidy and clean and half your work is done already.

Herbs are the difference between a dish tasting OK... and tasting eccellente. A sprinkle of the right leaves can take a dish into the sublime and every kitchen windowsill should have a row of pots: basil, rosemary and oregano, at the very least. They're easy to grow, they bring a bit of the garden into the house and they save Mama trailing outside all the time.

1. Keep your pantry well stocked in the basics: flour, oil, sugar, olives, Arborio rice, penne, spaghetti... and plenty of eggs, milk and cheese in the refrigerator. You'll always have the means to create something good to eat.

2. When it comes to olive oil, buy the best you can afford. A cheap oil can ruin good cooking.

3. Plan your meals for the week. Taking 15 minutes every Sunday night to organize yourself will save money, save time and save throwing food away needlessly.

Mama, I love the vanilla flavour in my panna cotta!

Grow what you can. Fresh insalata made from lettuce, rocket, spinach and tomatoes costs nothing — and tastes like pure Italian sunshine.

Take control. Roma had only one emperor: and so must your household. There's no democracy in the kitchen: Mama's in charge and that's final.

Manage your time: you only have one pair of hands, one pair of legs and one pair of eyes. My son Alessandro talks about something called 'multi-tasking' — it sounds like making life unnecessarily complicated to me. My mama didn't multi-task, and neither did her mama. Do one thing at a time, and do it well.

Insalata di fagioli bicolore
Green and white bean salad

serves 4

115 g/4 oz dried cannellini
  beans, soaked overnight
225 g/8 oz French beans,
  topped and tailed
1/4 red onion, thinly sliced
12 black olives, stoned
1 tbsp chopped chives

dressing
1/2 tbsp lemon juice
1/2 tsp Dijon mustard
6 tbsp extra virgin olive oil
salt and pepper

Drain the soaked beans and put in a saucepan with plenty of fresh water to cover. Bring to the boil, then boil rapidly for 15 minutes. Reduce the heat slightly and cook for a further 30 minutes, or until tender but not disintegrating. Add salt in the last 5 minutes of cooking. Drain and set aside.

Meanwhile, bring a large saucepan of water to the boil, plunge the French beans into the water, return to the boil and cook for 4 minutes, until just tender but still brightly coloured and crunchy. Drain and set aside. Whisk together the dressing ingredients, then leave to stand.

While both types of bean are still slightly warm, tip them into a shallow serving dish or arrange on individual warmed plates. Scatter over the onion slices, olives and chives. Whisk the dressing again and spoon over the salad.

Serve immediately, at room temperature.

Olio e sale alla barese
Tomato salad with cucumber

serves 4

1 small cucumber, peeled
2 beef tomatoes
1 onion
4 tbsp olive oil
2 tbsp white wine vinegar
2 slices white country bread
salt and pepper

Thinly slice the cucumber and tomatoes and place them in a salad bowl. Slice the onion into fine rings, then toss them with the cucumber and tomatoes.

Whisk together the oil and vinegar, season with salt and pepper and pour over the salad. Marinate for 20 minutes.

Toast the bread slices on both sides under a grill or in the oven until golden brown, then cut into bite-sized pieces. Toss them into the salad and serve immediately.

Insalata di pollo
Braised chicken salad

serves 4

3 tbsp olive oil
1 chicken, about 1.3 kg/3 lb
225 ml/8 fl oz dry white wine
1 onion, chopped
1 carrot, chopped
1 celery stick, chopped
1 fresh bay leaf
salt and pepper

Preheat the oven to 180°C/350°F/Gas Mark 4. Heat the olive oil in an ovenproof casserole over a medium–high heat. Add the chicken and fry for 15 minutes, turning, until golden all over. Pour in the wine and simmer for 2 minutes, then add the onion, carrot, celery and bay leaf. Season with salt and pepper. Cover tightly and transfer to the oven. Bake for 45–50 minutes, turning every 20 minutes, until the juices from the thickest part of the thigh run clear when pierced with a skewer. Discard the liquid and solids. When cool enough to handle, remove and discard the skin.

Strip the meat from the bone, slicing any large chunks into bite-sized pieces.

Arrange the chicken in a dish. Sprinkle with a little salt, a few peppercorns and the bay leaves. Pour in enough oil to coat generously. Cover tightly with clingfilm and marinate in the refrigerator for 1–2 days.

Remove the chicken from the refrigerator 2 hours before serving. Place in a colander set over a bowl to drain, and leave to stand until the oil has liquefied.

To make the salad, chop the leaves as desired. Combine the spinach, celery and chicory in a large serving dish. Toss with salt, enough oil from the chicken to just coat the leaves, and the wine vinegar. Arrange the chicken on top, discarding the peppercorns and bay leaves. Sprinkle with the balsamic vinegar before serving.

marinade
1 tsp black peppercorns
4 fresh bay leaves
125 ml/4 fl oz olive oil
salt

salad
150 g/5½ oz baby spinach
  leaves
5 young celery sticks
1 head chicory
1 tsp wine vinegar
1 tsp balsamic vinegar
salt

Insalata di prosciutto, salami e fichi
Ham and salami salad with figs

serves 6

9-12 ripe figs, depending on size
6 thin slices prosciutto
12 thin slices salami
1 small bunch fresh basil,
  separated into small sprigs
few fresh mint sprigs
1 small bunch rocket
2 tbsp freshly squeezed
  lemon juice
4 tbsp extra virgin olive oil
salt and pepper

Trim the stems of the figs to leave just a short length, then cut the figs into quarters.

Arrange the ham and salami on a large serving platter. Wash and dry the herbs and rocket and put in a bowl with the prepared figs.

Whisk the lemon juice and oil together with a fork in a small bowl and season well with salt and pepper.

Pour over the herbs and rocket and carefully turn them with the figs in the dressing until they are well coated.

Spoon the figs and leaves onto the meat and arrange around the platter.

Antipasti misti di carne
Mixed antipasti meat platter

Italian Prosciutto di Parma

serves 4

1 cantaloupe melon
55 g/2 oz Italian salami,
    thinly sliced
8 slices prosciutto
8 slices bresaola
8 slices mortadella
4 plum tomatoes, thinly sliced
4 fresh figs, quartered
55 g/2 oz black olives, stoned
2 tbsp shredded fresh
    basil leaves
4 tbsp extra virgin olive oil,
    plus extra to serve
pepper
sliced ciabatta loaf, to serve

Cut the melon in half, scoop out and discard the seeds, then cut the flesh into 8 wedges. Arrange the wedges on one half of a large serving platter.

Arrange the salami, prosciutto, bresaola and mortadella in loose folds on the other half of the platter. Arrange the tomato slices and fig quarters along the centre of the platter.

Sprinkle the olives and basil over the platter and drizzle with oil. Season to taste with pepper, then serve with slices of ciabatta and extra oil, for dipping and drizzling.

Salami Sausage

Black Olive

Bruschetta ai funghi selvatici
Wild mushroom bruschetta

serves 4

4 slices sourdough bread,
  such as Pugliese
3 garlic cloves, 1 halved and
  2 crushed
2 tbsp extra virgin olive oil
225 g/8 oz mixed wild mushrooms,
  such as ceps, chanterelles
  and field
1 tbsp olive oil
2 tbsp butter
1 small onion or 2 shallots,
  finely chopped
125 ml/4 fl oz dry white wine
  or Marsala
salt and pepper
2 tbsp coarsely chopped fresh
  flat-leaf parsley, to garnish

Toast the bread slices on both sides under a preheated grill or in a preheated ridged griddle pan, then rub with the garlic halves and drizzle with the extra virgin olive oil. Transfer to a baking sheet and keep warm in a warm oven. Wipe the mushrooms thoroughly to remove any trace of soil, and slice any large ones. Heat the olive oil with half the butter in a frying pan, then add the mushrooms and cook over a medium heat, stirring frequently, for 3—4 minutes, or until soft. Remove with a slotted spoon and keep warm in the oven.

Heat the remaining butter in the pan, add the onion and crushed garlic, then cook over a medium heat, stirring frequently, for 3—4 minutes, or until soft. Add the wine and stir well, then leave to bubble for 2—3 minutes, or until reduced and thickened. Return the mushrooms to the pan and heat through. The sauce should be thick enough to glaze the mushrooms.

Season to taste with salt and pepper. Pile the mushrooms on top of the warm bruschetta, then garnish with the parsley and serve immediately.

Funghi ripieni con spinaci e pancetta
Mushrooms stuffed with bacon and spinach

serves 4

55 g/2 oz fresh baby spinach
leaves
4 field mushrooms
3 tbsp olive oil
55 g/2 oz rindless bacon,
finely diced
2 garlic cloves, crushed
55 g/2 oz fresh white breadcrumbs
or brown breadcrumbs
2 tbsp chopped fresh basil
salt and pepper

Preheat the oven to 200°C/400°F/Gas Mark 6. Rinse the spinach and place in a saucepan with just the water clinging to the leaves. Cook for 2—3 minutes, until wilted. Drain, squeezing out as much liquid as possible, and finely chop. Cut the stalks from the mushrooms and finely chop, reserving the whole caps.

Heat 2 tablespoons of the oil in a frying pan. Add the mushroom caps, rounded-side down, and cook for 1 minute. Remove from the pan and arrange, rounded-side down, in a large ovenproof dish. Add the chopped mushroom stalks, bacon and garlic to the pan and cook for 5 minutes.

Stir in the spinach, breadcrumbs, basil, and salt and pepper to taste. Mix well and divide the stuffing between the mushroom caps. Drizzle the remaining oil over the top. Bake in the preheated oven for 20 minutes, until crisp and golden.

Mama's Tip
Little nuggets of bacon
with chopped spinach,
garlic and crisp, golden
breadcrumbs make a
delicious stuffing for
oven-baked mushrooms.
They can be served
straight from the oven,
or prepared ahead of
time and served at room
temperature.

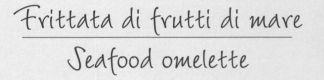

Frittata di frutti di mare
Seafood omelette

serves 3

2 tbsp unsalted butter
1 tbsp olive oil
1 onion, very finely chopped
175 g/6 oz courgettes, halved
   lengthways and sliced
1 celery stick, very
   finely chopped
85 g/3 oz button mushrooms,
   sliced
55 g/2 oz French beans, cut into
   5-cm/2-inch lengths
4 eggs
85 g/3 oz mascarpone cheese
1 tbsp chopped fresh thyme
1 tbsp shredded fresh basil
200 g/7 oz canned tuna,
   drained and flaked
115 g/4 oz shelled cooked prawns
salt and pepper

Melt the butter with the oil in a heavy-based frying pan with a flameproof handle. If the pan has a wooden handle, protect it with foil because it needs to go under the grill. Add the onion and cook over a low heat, stirring occasionally, for 5 minutes, until soft.

Add the courgettes, celery, mushrooms and beans and cook, stirring occasionally, for a further 8—10 minutes, until starting to brown.

Beat the eggs with the mascarpone cheese, thyme, basil, and salt and pepper to taste.

Add the tuna to the pan and stir it into the mixture with a wooden spoon. Add the prawns. Pour the egg mixture into the pan and cook for 5 minutes, until it is just starting to set. Draw the egg from the sides of the pan towards the centre to allow the uncooked egg to run underneath.

Put the pan under a preheated grill and cook until the egg is just set and the surface is starting to brown. Cut the omelette into wedges and serve.

Spaghetti con le polpette
Spaghetti with meatballs

serves 6

1 potato, diced
400 g/14 oz beef mince
1 onion, finely chopped
1 egg
4 tbsp chopped fresh flat-leaf
  parsley
plain flour, for dusting
5 tbsp virgin olive oil
400 ml/14 fl oz passata
2 tbsp tomato purée
400 g/14 oz dried spaghetti
salt and pepper
6 shredded fresh basil leaves
  and freshly grated Parmesan
  cheese, to garnish

Place the potato in a small saucepan, add cold water to cover and a pinch of salt, and bring to the boil. Cook for 10—15 minutes, until tender, then drain. Either mash thoroughly with a potato masher or fork or pass through a potato ricer.

Combine the potato, mince, onion, egg and parsley in a bowl and season to taste with salt and pepper. Spread out the flour on a plate. With dampened hands, shape the meat mixture into walnut-sized balls and roll in the flour. Shake off any excess.

Heat the oil in a heavy-based frying pan, add the meatballs and cook over a medium heat, stirring and turning frequently, for 8—10 minutes, until golden all over. Add the passata and tomato purée and cook for a further 10 minutes, until the sauce is reduced and thickened. Meanwhile, bring a large saucepan of lightly salted water to the boil. Add the pasta, bring back to the boil and cook for 8—10 minutes, until tender but still firm to the bite.

Drain well and add to the meatball sauce, tossing well to coat. Transfer to a warmed serving dish, garnish with the basil leaves and grated Parmesan cheese and serve immediately.

Bocconcini di pollo pastellati
Chicken morsels fried in batter

serves 6-8

500 g/1 lb 2 oz skinless,
    boneless chicken thighs
3 tbsp olive oil
juice of 1/2 lemon
2 garlic cloves, crushed
8 tbsp plain flour
vegetable oil, for deep-frying
2 eggs, beaten
salt and pepper
coarsely chopped fresh flat-leaf
    parsley, to garnish
lemon wedges, to serve

Cut the chicken thighs into 4-cm/1½-inch chunks. Mix the olive oil, lemon juice, garlic, and salt and pepper in a bowl. Add the chicken pieces and leave to marinate at room temperature for an hour, or overnight in the refrigerator.

Spread the flour on a plate and mix with a pinch of salt and plenty of pepper.

When ready to cook, remove the chicken pieces from the marinade and drain.

Heat the vegetable oil in a deep-fat fryer or large saucepan to 180°C/350°F, or until a cube of bread browns in 30 seconds. Roll the chicken in the seasoned flour and then in the beaten egg. Immediately drop into the hot oil, a few pieces at a time, and deep-fry for about 5 minutes, until golden and crisp, turning occasionally with tongs. Drain on crumpled kitchen paper. Place the chicken pieces in a warmed serving dish and sprinkle with parsley. Serve hot, with thick wedges of lemon.

Tonno con fagioli bianchi e carciofi
Seared tuna with white beans and artichokes

serves 6

150 ml/5 fl oz extra virgin
   olive oil
juice of 1 lemon
½ tsp dried chilli flakes
4 thin fresh tuna steaks,
   weighing about 450 g/1 lb
300 g/10½ oz dried cannellini
   beans, soaked overnight
1 shallot, finely chopped
1 garlic clove, crushed
2 tsp finely chopped rosemary
2 tbsp chopped flat-leaf parsley
4 oil-cured artichokes, quartered
4 vine-ripened tomatoes, sliced
   lengthways into segments
16 black olives, stoned
salt and pepper
lemon wedges, to garnish

Put 4 tablespoons of the oil in a shallow dish with 3 tablespoons of the lemon juice, the chilli flakes, and ¼ teaspoon of pepper. Add the tuna steaks and leave to marinate at room temperature for 1 hour, turning occasionally.

Meanwhile, drain the beans and put in a saucepan with plenty of fresh water to cover. Bring to the boil, then boil rapidly for 15 minutes. Reduce the heat slightly and cook for another 30 minutes, or until tender but not disintegrating. Add salt in the last 5 minutes of cooking. Drain the beans and place in a bowl. While still warm, toss with 5 tablespoons of the olive oil, then stir in the shallot, garlic, rosemary, parsley and remaining lemon juice.

Season to taste with salt and pepper. Leave to stand for at least
30 minutes to allow the flavours to develop. Heat the remaining
oil in a frying pan until hot. Add the tuna and the marinade
and sear for 1—2 minutes on each side over a very high heat.
Remove from the pan and leave to cool a little.

Transfer the beans to a serving dish. Mix in the artichokes,
tomatoes and olives, adding more oil and seasoning if necessary.
Flake the tuna and arrange on top. Garnish with lemon
wedges and serve at room temperature.

43

Capesante al forno
Baked scallops

serves 6

700 g/1 lb 9 oz shelled scallops,
  chopped
2 onions, finely chopped
2 garlic cloves, finely chopped
3 tbsp chopped fresh parsley
pinch of freshly grated nutmeg
pinch of ground cloves
2 tbsp fresh white breadcrumbs
2 tbsp olive oil
salt and pepper

Preheat the oven to 200°C/400°F/Gas Mark 6. Mix the scallops, onions, garlic, 2 tablespoons of the parsley, the nutmeg and cloves together in a bowl and season to taste with salt and pepper.

Divide the mixture between 4 scrubbed scallop shells or heatproof dishes. Sprinkle the breadcrumbs and remaining parsley on top and drizzle with the olive oil.

Bake the scallops in the preheated oven for 15—20 minutes, or until lightly golden and piping hot. Serve immediately.

Mama's tips for feeding a big family

Remember, Mama's the boss! When you're feeding a big family, you can't bend to their every individual whim: Casa Mama is not a ristorante, there is no menu to choose from!

Families are the root of all Italian life. They make us everything we are. I was one of seven children, and Alberto, my husband, the eldest of five. Now we have six children of our own, and more grandchildren than I have fingers on my hands and toes on both feet together. A big family is a gift from Heaven — and a big dining table is where we all come together to show our thanks for such a blessing.

My mama had a saying: 'È meglio un uovo oggi che una gallina domani' – an egg today is better than a chicken tomorrow.

Even if you don't have much, using what you do have with passion and imagination can still be enough for a feast.

Cut your coat according to your cloth. Many hungry mouths can take a lot of feeding — and keeping everyone full and happy means learning to budget.

A big pot will feed more than many individual servings — and good ciabatta will pad out any spaces left by a smaller pot.

Make mealtimes the focal point of the day. Everyone should sit, eat, drink, talk and laugh together. From the oldest mama to the youngest bambino, meals are there to be shared: and there should be no excuses for missing them.

When you're cooking for many, keep it simple. When we have the children, grandchildren, cousins, nephews, nieces and even grandcousins for dinner, two or three simple dishes done well — a big salad, maybe, and spaghetti with meatballs — are easier for Mama to handle and there's less washing-up for Alberto!

Panna cotta
Panna cotta

Cut the vanilla pod lengthways and scrape out the seeds. In a saucepan, bring the cream to the boil with the vanilla pod and seeds. Stir in the caster sugar. Simmer over a low heat for 15 minutes.

Soak the gelatine in cold water for about 10 minutes, then drain or press the liquid from the gelatine. Pour the hot cream through a sieve into a bowl, then dissolve the gelatine in it.

Rinse 4 small soufflé dishes in cold water and fill with the cream. Chill overnight in the refrigerator. Wash the strawberries, setting aside a few for decoration. Cook the remaining strawberries with the icing sugar. While hot, press the berries through a sieve into a bowl and then leave to cool. To serve, turn out the soufflé dishes onto dessert plates, top with strawberry sauce and decorate with the reserved whole berries.

serves 4

1 vanilla pod
475 ml/17 fl oz double cream
4½ tbsp caster sugar
4 sheets clear gelatine
500 g/1 lb 2 oz strawberries
3 tbsp icing sugar

Macedonia
Fruit salad

Stone the plums and nectarines and cut into thin wedges. Peel and quarter the pears, remove the cores and cut into cubes. Place the fruit in a bowl and sprinkle with the lime juice.

Halve the grapes and remove any seeds with the point of a knife. Combine the caster sugar and vanilla sugar with the orange juice and amaretto. Pour this over the fruit and gently toss so all the fruit is coated. Chill in the refrigerator for 1 hour.

Quarter the figs and place in a bowl with the fruit salad. Serve.

serves 4

5 large black plums
2 nectarines
2 pears
juice of 1 lime
200 g/7 oz red grapes
200 g/7 oz white grapes
2 tbsp caster sugar
2 tsp vanilla sugar
7 tbsp freshly squeezed orange juice
60 ml/2¼ fl oz amaretto
2 fresh figs

Gelato di albicocche
Apricot ice cream

serves 6

500 g/1 lb 2 oz ripe apricots
300 ml/10 fl oz single cream
175 g/6 oz caster sugar
200 ml/7 fl oz milk
½ tsp vanilla extract

Mama's Tip
If you have an ice-cream maker,
pour the mixture into the machine
and freeze according to the
manufacturer's instructions.

Halve the apricots and remove and discard the stones. Put the apricots in a food processor or blender and process until smooth.

Whip the cream and sugar together in a mixing bowl using a hand-held electric mixer or a hand whisk, until the sugar has dissolved. Whisk in the apricot purée, milk and vanilla extract. Pour into a lidded freezerproof container, then cover and freeze for 1 hour. Remove from the freezer and whisk thoroughly, using a hand-held electric mixer or a hand whisk. Re-cover and freeze for a further hour.

Repeat the whisking and freezing process until the mixture is almost frozen solid. Whisk a final time, then re-cover and return to the freezer until required.

Transfer the ice cream to the refrigerator 15 minutes before serving to soften slightly.

Be my

Valentines

Mama's Celebrations

When it's time for a party in our part of Apulia, the only person allowed to create the party food is Mama. Celebration feasts are as intrinsic to Italian life as *vino rosso* and opera and Mass on a Sunday... and laying on the right food, cooked the right way, is all-important.

From Mama's famous *risotti* and *osso buco* to unbeatable recipes for chicken, turkey and duck, the following pages will cover any party, big or small... and Mama's handy tips on 'big meal' equipment will prevent any last-minute panics.

Leaving your guests with full bellies and smiles on their faces can be easier than you think — let Mama show you how!

Risotto con gli aspargi
Risotto with asparagus

serves 4

500 g/1 lb 2 oz asparagus
1 litre/1¾ pints water
1 pinch sugar
3 tbsp. butter
1 small onion, finely chopped
300 g/10½ oz risotto rice
125 ml/4 fl oz white wine
salt and pepper

Remove the woody ends of the asparagus. Cut off the tips and set them aside. Cut the rest of the asparagus into pieces. Bring the water to the boil in a saucepan with the sugar, 1 teaspoon of the butter and a little salt. Blanch the asparagus tips briefly. Remove them with a slotted spoon, refresh in iced water and set aside. Put the asparagus pieces in the cooking liquid and cook them for 15 minutes. Pour the liquid through a sieve, saving the broth. Purée the asparagus with a hand-held electric mixer and set aside to keep warm.

Heat 1 tablespoon of butter in a large frying pan, add the onion and sauté. Add the rice, stirring to coat with butter, then deglaze the pan with the wine. As soon as the wine has evaporated, pour in one third of the hot asparagus broth, stirring constantly until it is absorbed. Repeat twice. After a cooking time of about 15 minutes, add the remaining butter and the asparagus purée, and blend the asparagus tips into the rice. Season to taste with salt and pepper. Remove from the heat, cover and leave to rest for 2—3 minutes before serving.

Risotto nero con seppie
Black risotto with squid

serves 4

500 g/1 lb 2 oz squid
1 bunch flat-leaf parsley
4 tbsp olive oil
1 shallot, finely chopped
1 garlic clove, finely chopped
300 g/10½ oz risotto rice
225 ml/8 fl oz white wine
1 litre/1¾ pints fish stock
salt and pepper

Clean the squid and carefully remove the ink sac from each one. Cut the squid into narrow strips. Cut the stems off the parsley and finely chop the leaves. Bring a small quantity of water to the boil and cook the ink sacs with the parsley stems and a pinch of salt for several minutes. Pass through a sieve and save the liquid. Heat the olive oil in a saucepan, add the shallot and garlic and sauté. Add the strips of squid and sauté briefly. Stir in the rice and coat with the oil. Deglaze the pan with the white wine.

Heat the stock in another saucepan. As soon as the wine has evaporated, gradually pour in one third of the hot stock, stirring constantly until the liquid is absorbed. Repeat this process twice more.

After about 15 minutes, stir in the ink sauce and simmer for a few minutes. Season to taste with salt and pepper and serve sprinkled with the reserved chopped parsley.

Risotto ai funghi porcini
Risotto with ceps

serves 4

300 g/10½ oz ceps
75 g/2¾ oz prosciutto
3 tbsp butter
2 shallots, finely chopped
300 g/10½ oz risotto rice
225 ml/8 fl oz prosecco
1 litre/1¾ pints meat stock
salt and pepper
1 tbsp fresh finely chopped parsley,
    to garnish
75 g/2¾ oz grated Parmesan cheese, to serve

Clean and thinly slice the ceps. Finely
dice the prosciutto. Melt half the butter
in a saucepan, add the shallots and
prosciutto and fry. Sprinkle the rice into
the pan and continue to cook. Deglaze the
pan with the prosecco.
    Heat the stock in a separate saucepan.
When the wine has nearly evaporated, pour
in one third of the hot stock, stirring
constantly, until the liquid is absorbed.
Repeat twice more.
    Meanwhile, melt the remaining butter in
a saucepan, add the mushrooms, sauté, then
add to the risotto. Season with salt and
pepper. Sprinkle with parsley and serve
with Parmesan cheese.

57

Mama's tips for the perfect 'big Italian gathering'

A celebration without good food is like a summer without sunshine — possible for the English, maybe, but in Apulia almost unthinkable. Nobody does a celebratory feast like the Italians: and nobody in Italy does it like Mama.

And with a little help, you can put on a spread your friends and family will remember for years.

It's not just about the food. Good wine, good conversation, laughter, music and stories are all essential ingredients.

As much as possible, seat people where everyone can see everyone else. Borrow and improvise: push tables together to make bigger tables. With good clean tablecloths and plenty to eat nobody will know any different.

Include the children. Why do some people insist on the little ones eating separately? To Mama that's against nature. With children at the table there is always more joy.

Don't forget about drink. Plenty of vino, big jugs of icy acqua, fresh orange juice for the children... thirsty guests are unhappy guests and at *Casa Mama* it's Alberto's job to make sure nobody ever has an empty glass.

Mama's celebrations are all-inclusive affairs. My guests don't sit and wait to be served – some help Mama in the kitchen, some help Alberto with the *vino*. Others play games with the children, or entertain each other with music, songs, jokes and stories. A big Italian gathering is not like going to a *ristorante*: it is a noisy, busy, living thing where everyone is involved.

There is an Italian proverb: 'Chi mangia da solo, muore da solo' — he who eats alone, dies alone. Food is best enjoyed in company: don't save your big gatherings for special occasions — being alive and with people you love is cause enough for celebration.

Don't worry too much about good etiquette. Basic manners are important, of course, but the essential thing is that everyone enjoys themselves. Who cares what fork is used, really?

CENTENAIRE
TIMBRE-POSTE FR
GRAND PALAIS

SOUVENIR DE LA TOUR EIFFEL

Construite de 1887 à 1889. Hauteur : 300 m.
Poids : 7 millions de kilos. Ecartement à la
base : 104 m. 2.500 000 rivets relient ses 15.000
pièces de métal. La 1re plate-forme est à 57 m,
la 2e à 115 m. La 3e à 280 m. Les escaliers
portent 1.710 marches.

59

Melanzane alla campagnola
Country-style marinated aubergine slices

serves 4

4 aubergines
6 tomatoes
2 garlic cloves
½ bunch fresh parsley
4 tbsp olive oil,
    plus extra for greasing
salt and pepper

Wash and trim the aubergines, then cut into slices ⅓ inch/1 cm thick. Salt them and place them in a sieve to drain for 1 hour.

Preheat the oven to 200°C/400°F/Gas Mark 6. Meanwhile, peel and quarter the tomatoes, remove the seeds and finely dice the flesh. Peel the garlic and finely chop, along with the parsley. Add this mixture to the tomatoes, then add salt and pepper to taste. Stir in 2 tablespoons of the olive oil and leave to marinate.

Lightly oil a baking sheet. Pat the aubergine slices dry with kitchen paper and arrange them next to each other on the prepared baking sheet. Drizzle over the remaining oil, then roast them in the oven for 5 minutes on each side. Brush the aubergine slices with the tomato mixture and stack them up into little towers to serve.

Mama's Celebrations

Polenta e fontina
Polenta with fontina

serves 4

1 tsp salt
140 g/5 oz coarsely ground
  polenta
4 tbsp butter,
  plus extra for greasing
175 g/6 oz fontina cheese
freshly ground white pepper

Put 1 litre/1³/4 pints of water in a large saucepan with the salt and bring to the boil. Add the polenta, stirring constantly, and cook for 5 minutes. Reduce the heat and leave the polenta to simmer for about 30 minutes, stirring constantly, until it no longer sticks to the pan.

Rinse a round baking dish with cold water. Transfer the polenta to the dish, spread it smooth and leave to cool. Remove it from the dish and slice through it twice, horizontally, to give three even layers. Clean the baking dish and grease it with butter.

Preheat the oven to 200°C/400°F/Gas Mark 6. Thinly slice the cheese. Lay a slice of polenta in the baking dish. Top it with a third of the cheese slices, season with pepper, then cover with the next slice of polenta. Repeat, then spread the remaining cheese on top. Place little dabs of butter over it. Bake in the preheated oven for 20—25 minutes.

Osso buco alla Milanese
Milanese-style osso buco

serves 4

4 slices veal shank,
    each 4 cm/1½ inches thick
flour, for coating
3½ tbsp butter
125 ml/4 fl oz white wine
400 g/14 oz canned tomatoes
1 garlic clove
1 tbsp grated lemon peel
2 tbsp finely chopped fresh
    parsley
salt and pepper

Wash the veal slices and pat dry with kitchen paper. Rub with salt and pepper and coat with flour, shaking off any excess.

Melt the butter in a deep saucepan and brown the veal slices on both sides. Deglaze the pan with the wine, then reduce. Stir in the tomatoes and season with salt and pepper. Cover the pan and stew the meat over a low heat for at least 1½ hours, turning the slices over several times in the tomato sauce as they cook.

When the meat begins to separate from the bone, it is done. Finely chop the garlic and combine it with the lemon peel and parsley. Sprinkle over the sliced meat just before serving.

Involtini alla Barese
Beef roulades with pecorino

serves 4

8 thin slices of beef,
    100 g/3½ oz each
55 g/2 oz stoned green olives
8 slices coppa ham
85 g/3 oz medium-aged pecorino
    cheese, shaved
2 tbsp olive oil
1 onion, finely chopped
1 garlic clove, finely chopped
1 tbsp tomato purée
125 ml/4 fl oz dry red wine
225 ml/8 fl oz beef stock
1 sprig sage
salt and pepper

Wash the sliced beef, pat it dry with kitchen paper and pound flat.

Finely dice the olives. Lightly season the meat with salt and pepper on both sides and cover each slice with a slice of ham. Sprinkle the olives and cheese over the ham.

Roll up the roulades and tie them with kitchen string.

Heat the oil in a saucepan and brown the roulades over a medium heat. Add the onion, garlic and tomato purée and sauté.

Deglaze the pan with the wine, stirring to loosen the residue, and leave the liquid to reduce.

Pour in the stock, add the sage sprig, half cover the pan and braise for 30—40 minutes over a low heat. Take the roulades out of the pan, remove the string and keep the meat warm. Bring the sauce to the boil and season to taste with salt and pepper. Serve the roulades on warmed plates with sauce poured over them.

Stracotto di manzo
Beef braised in red wine

serves 6

3 tbsp olive oil
2 onions, finely sliced
2 garlic cloves, chopped
1 kg/2 lb 4 oz stewing steak,
    cut into thick strips
2 tbsp plain flour
300 ml/10 fl oz good-quality red
    wine, such as Chianti
2 fresh sage sprigs
225 ml/8 fl oz beef stock or
    vegetable stock
1 tbsp tomato purée
salt and pepper
1 tbsp finely chopped fresh
    flat-leaf parsley, to garnish
cooked seasonal green vegetables,
    to serve (optional)

Preheat the oven to 150°C/300°F/Gas Mark 2. Heat 1 tablespoon of the oil in a large frying pan, then add the onions and garlic and cook over a medium heat, stirring frequently, for 6—8 minutes, or until soft and brown.

Remove with a slotted spoon and transfer to a casserole.

Heat the remaining oil in the pan, then add the steak strips and cook over a high heat, stirring, for 3—4 minutes, or until brown all over. Sprinkle in the flour and stir well to prevent lumps.

Season well with salt and pepper. Reduce the heat to medium, then pour in the wine, stirring constantly, and bring to the boil, continuing to stir.

Carefully turn the contents of the pan into the casserole. Add the sage, stock and tomato purée, then cover and cook in the centre of the preheated oven for 2½—3 hours. Remove from the oven and discard the sage, then taste and adjust the seasoning if necessary.

Serve immediately, sprinkled with parsley, and with some green vegetables, if using.

Mama's Tip
A lamb casserole can be made in the same way. Use lean leg or shoulder of lamb. Sometimes tougher cuts of meat are braised in Tuscan cooking, quite often on the hob. But here the beef is cooked in the oven so that it needs little attention.

Spezzatino di maiale
Pork stew

serves 4

600 g/1 lb 5 oz lean pork
2–3 tbsp olive oil
1 tsp fennel seeds
5 garlic cloves, finely chopped
1 fresh red chilli,
    finely chopped
300 g/10½ oz tomatoes,
    peeled and diced
salt and pepper
fresh basil, to garnish

Wash the meat, pat dry with kitchen paper and cut into bite-sized pieces. Heat the oil in a casserole and add the fennel seeds and garlic.

Season the meat with salt and pepper.

Brown the meat on all sides in the hot oil. As soon as the meat browns, add the chilli and tomatoes. Cover and stew over a low heat for about 1 hour, adding a little warm water as needed.

loin

spare rib

leg

hock

blade

belly

Pollo alla cacciatora
Chicken cacciatore

serves 4

1 chicken
2 tbsp olive oil
55 g/2 oz pancetta, diced
1 onion, finely chopped
125 ml/4 fl oz white wine
4 tomatoes
225 ml/8 fl oz meat stock
salt and pepper

Wash the chicken, pat dry with kitchen paper and cut into 8 pieces. Rub generous amounts of salt and pepper into the skin. Heat the oil in a casserole, add the pancetta and onion and fry until the onions are translucent.

Add the chicken pieces and brown on all sides. Deglaze the casserole with the white wine and leave to simmer for 5 minutes.

Peel and quarter the tomatoes, remove the seeds and cut into small dice. Add to the chicken, then pour in the stock. Cover and cook over a low heat for 30—40 minutes. Season to taste with salt and pepper before serving.

Involtini di petti di pollo
Stuffed chicken breasts

serves 4

4 skinless, boneless chicken
  breasts, each weighing about
  150 g/5½ oz
4 thin slices prosciutto
4 slices pecorino cheese
4 cooked asparagus spears,
  plus extra to serve
1 tbsp plain flour
3 tbsp butter
2 tbsp olive oil
150 ml/5 fl oz dry white wine
50 ml/2 fl oz chicken stock
salt and pepper

Put each chicken breast between two sheets of clingfilm or inside a polythene food bag and, using a rolling pin, gently beat out until 8 mm/³/8 inch thick. Season well with salt and pepper and place a slice of ham on top of each breast.

Top each with a slice of cheese and an asparagus spear. Roll up carefully and secure with fine string. Dust with flour and season well with salt and pepper.

Heat 2 tablespoons of the butter with the oil in a large frying pan. Add the chicken rolls and cook over a medium heat, turning frequently, for 15 minutes, or until cooked through, tender and golden brown. Remove the string, then transfer the chicken rolls to a warmed serving dish and keep warm.

Add the wine and stock to the pan and bring to the boil, scraping up and stirring in any residue from the base of the pan. Add the remaining butter, stir well and leave to bubble until thick.

Spoon the sauce over the chicken and serve immediately, with extra asparagus spears.

Mama's Tip
You could use Marsala instead of white wine to give a different flavour.

Anatra con verdure
Duck with vegetables

serves 4-6

1 young duck, about 1.4 kg/3 lb
1 onion
1 bay leaf
3 cloves
1 bouquet garni
5 allspice berries
450 g/1 lb carrots
450 g/1 lb thick parsley root
2 tbsp olive oil
225 ml/8 fl oz veal stock
2 tbsp finely chopped parsley
salt and pepper

Wash the duck and place it in a large saucepan. Spike the onion with the bay leaf and cloves, then add it and the bouquet garni to the pan. Add enough water to cover the duck completely. Add salt and pepper and the allspice berries.

Bring to the boil, skimming off the foam that forms on the surface, and simmer over a low heat for about 1¼ hours. Cut the carrots and parsley roots into pieces of equal size. Heat the olive oil in a saucepan, add the vegetables and sauté, then pour over the stock, cover the pan and cook for 10 minutes. Season with salt and pepper and mix in the parsley. Keep the vegetables warm.

Remove the duck from the broth and leave to drain well. Remove the skin. Bone the breast meat and legs, then slice. Serve the duck meat and vegetables on a warmed serving platter, or in individual bowls.

Vongole veraci marinate
Marinated clams

serves 4

1 kg/2 lb 4 oz fresh clams
1 onion
2 garlic cloves
90 ml/3 fl oz olive oil
225 ml/8 fl oz dry white wine
1 tbsp finely chopped parsley
juice of ½ lemon
salt and pepper

Scrub the clam shells. Soak them in cold water for 1 hour, changing the water several times. Discard any clams that have open shells. Peel the onion and garlic and finely dice.

Heat 2 tablespoons of the oil in a large saucepan, add the onion and garlic and sauté until translucent. Deglaze the pan with the wine and bring to the boil. Add the clams, cover and cook over a high heat for 3—4 minutes, shaking the pan several times.

Remove the clams from the pan with a slotted spoon, discarding any that have not opened and place in a bowl. Stir in the parsley, lemon juice and remaining olive oil, and season with salt and pepper. Marinate for 30 minutes, then serve.

Carciofi e frutti di mare
Artichokes with seafood

serves 4

4-6 small young artichokes
juice of 2 lemons
3 garlic cloves
50 ml/2 fl oz olive oil
125 ml/4 fl oz white wine
450 g/1 lb frozen, pre-cooked
    mixed seafood, thawed
300 g/10½ oz buffalo
    mozzarella cheese, sliced
salt and pepper
butter, for greasing

Clean the artichokes, cut the stems to a length of 4 cm/1½ inches and peel. Remove the tough, outer leaves and slice off the thistles from the inner leaves.

Fill a bowl with the water and add the lemon juice. Cut the artichokes lengthways into thin slices and immediately drop them into the lemon water.

Leave to soak for 10 minutes, then pour off the water and drain well. Cut the garlic into slices. Heat the olive oil in a non-stick saucepan and fry the garlic until golden brown, then remove and discard it.

Sauté the artichoke slices in the olive oil, stirring constantly. Season with salt and pepper, then add the white wine. Cover the pan and gently braise the artichokes over a medium heat for about 30 minutes, shaking the pan several times as they cook. Meanwhile, preheat the oven to 220°C/425°F/Gas Mark 7 and grease a baking dish with butter.

Place the artichoke slices in the prepared baking dish and pour over the cooking juices. Add the seafood and top with cheese slices. Bake in the preheated oven for 20–25 minutes, until the cheese starts to brown. Serve immediately.

Gamberi in padella
Pan-fried prawns

serves 4

4 garlic cloves
20–24 large, raw prawns, peeled
115 g/4-oz butter
4 tbsp olive oil
6 tbsp brandy
salt and pepper
2 tbsp chopped fresh parsley,
    to garnish
lemon wedges, to serve

Using a sharp knife, peel and slice the garlic.

Wash the prawns and pat dry with kitchen paper.

Melt the butter with the oil in a large frying pan, add the garlic and prawns and fry over a high heat, stirring, for 3—4 minutes, until the prawns are pink.

Add the brandy and season to taste with salt and pepper. Sprinkle with chopped parsley and serve immediately with lemon wedges.

Mama's essential 'big meal' equipment

Big meals mean big planning. Before you start to cook, get your kitchen organized, de-cluttered and free from interference from the likes of Alberto. Make a list of everything you need and lay it all out ready — down to the last spoon.

You can never have too many wooden spoons. I keep mine in two big old olive oil tins - one lot for sweet things, the other for savoury.

Love your knives. In the kitchen, you're nothing without your knives: they're not just for chopping, they're the tools with which you express your creativity and passion for food. Nurture them, keep them clean and sharp. Look after them like a sculptor looks after his chisels, like an artist looks after his brushes. Without them you're no cook at all.

Keep different chopping boards for different flavours. Mama keeps four: one for fish, one for meat, one for vegetables and a thick wooden one for bread and cheese.

Get the biggest baking dishes and roasting tins your oven can handle; and the best you can afford.

If you're cooking for friends, family and half the village like Mama seems to, they're worth their weight in gold.

Every cook should have at least one big stock pot. The best kind are the sort that can be used on the hob and in the oven – not only are they perfect for making the kinds of big wholesome stews that work so well for large numbers, but they mean that even with a small oven you can keep two on the go at once.

Remember, the best cooking equipment can't be found in the shops. Your senses are the truest guide of all: use your eyes, nose and, most important of all, your tastebuds.

Tiramisù bianco con fragole
White tiramisù with strawberries

serves 6

2 eggs, separated
150 g/5½ oz icing sugar,
    sifted
350 g/12 oz mascarpone cheese
6 tbsp milk
125 ml/4 fl oz Marsala
20 ladyfingers
40 g/1½ oz chopped almonds
55 g/2 oz white chocolate,
    coarsely grated
fresh strawberries, halved,
    to serve

Whisk the egg yolks with the sugar in a mixing bowl with a hand-held electric mixer or hand whisk until thick and creamy. Add the mascarpone cheese and whisk into the egg yolk mixture.

Whisk the egg whites in a separate mixing bowl and then fold into the mascarpone mixture.

Pour the milk into a shallow dish and add the Marsala. Dip the ladyfingers into the milk mixture just long enough to soften, then arrange half the dipped ladyfingers in the base of a glass or china dish about 23–25 cm/9–10 inches in diameter. Sprinkle over half the almonds. Spread over a third of the mascarpone mixture and top with a layer of the remaining dipped ladyfingers and the remaining nuts. Spoon the remaining mascarpone mixture over the top and swirl to give an attractive appearance. Cover with clingfilm and chill in the refrigerator for 2–3 hours.

To serve, remove from the refrigerator and decorate with the white chocolate and strawberries.

Pere con Marsala
Poached pears in Marsala

serves 4

4 firm dessert pears,
   such as Comice
55 g/2 oz caster sugar
2 cinnamon sticks
125 ml/4 fl oz Marsala
125 ml/4 fl oz soured cream,
   to serve

Carefully peel the pears. Cut a slice from the base of each pear and discard, then remove and discard the core from each base, using a pointed knife. Put the prepared pears in a saucepan, add enough water to just cover, then add the sugar and cinnamon sticks.

Slowly bring to the boil over a low heat, stirring until the sugar has dissolved. Cover and simmer gently until the pears are tender. This will take from 20—40 minutes, depending on their firmness. Remove from the heat.

Remove the pears with a slotted spoon and transfer to a serving dish. Remove the cinnamon sticks. Return the pan to the heat and leave the liquid to bubble for 2—3 minutes, or until thick. Stir in the Marsala and pour over the pears.

Serve warm or cover and leave to chill in the refrigerator before serving with soured cream.

Mama's Tip
Pears can also be poached in red wine or white wine.

Pears are a popular fruit in Tuscan cooking and are frequently served as part of a salad, often with walnuts and cheese. Here they are poached in Marsala until tender.

Panforte di Siena
Tuscan Christmas cake

serves 12-14

90 g/3¼ oz hazelnuts
115 g/4 oz almonds
85 g/3 oz candied peel
55 g/2 oz dried apricots,
    finely chopped
55 g/2 oz candied pineapple,
    finely chopped
grated rind of 1 orange
55 g/2 oz plain flour
2 tbsp cocoa powder
1 tsp ground cinnamon
1/4 tsp ground coriander
1/4 tsp freshly grated nutmeg
1/4 tsp ground cloves
115 g/4 oz caster sugar
175 g/6 oz clear honey
icing sugar, to decorate

Preheat the oven to 180°C/350°F/Gas Mark 4. Line a 20-cm/8-inch round springform cake tin with baking paper. Spread out the hazelnuts on a baking sheet and toast in the preheated oven for 10 minutes, until golden brown. Turn them onto a tea towel and rub off the skins. Meanwhile, spread out the almonds on a baking sheet and toast in the oven for 10 minutes, until golden, watching carefully, because they can burn easily.

Reduce the oven temperature to 150°C/300°F/Gas Mark 2. Chop all the nuts and place in a large bowl. Add the candied peel, apricots, pineapple and orange rind to the nuts and mix well. Sift the flour, cocoa, cinnamon, coriander, nutmeg and cloves together into the bowl and mix well.

Put the sugar and honey into a saucepan and set over a low heat, stirring, until the caster sugar has dissolved. Bring to the boil and cook for 5 minutes, until thickened and starting to darken. Stir the nut mixture into the pan and remove from the heat. Spoon the mixture into the prepared cake tin and level the surface with the back of a damp spoon. Bake in the oven for 1 hour, then transfer to a wire rack to cool in the tin. Carefully remove the cake from the tin and peel off the lining paper. Just before serving, dredge the top with icing sugar. Cut into thin wedges to serve.

Mama's Comfort Food

Cooking is not all about taking care of others — Mama loves to look after Alberto and the children, but she also has to look after herself! Comfort food is for those days when you're a little down, when you need cheering up… and also for the times when all you really want to do is relax with something easy to make and delicious to eat. Pizza, ravioli, frittata, a wholesome seafood stew — and a panettone bread-and-butter pudding to warm every bone in your body.

This chapter is Mama's *cibo per l'anima*: food for the soul.

My favourite pizzas

Basic pizza dough

2 sachets easy-blend
  dried yeast
½ tsp caster sugar
125 ml/4 fl oz lukewarm
  water
425 g/15 oz plain flour,
  plus extra for dusting
1 tsp salt
3 tbsp olive oil
5–7 tbsp water

Crumble the yeast into
a small bowl and sprinkle
with the sugar. Add
the water, then stir to
dissolve the yeast and
sugar. Cover with a clean
tea towel and prove in a
warm spot for 30 minutes.

Sift the flour into a
large bowl. Make a hollow
in the centre and pour
the yeast mixture, salt,
olive oil and the water
into it.

Knead everything into a
smooth, silky dough, then
shape it into a ball. Dust
the ball with a little
flour, cover and set aside
in a warm place to rise for
a further hour, or until
doubled in volume.

Pizza alla marinara
Mariner's pizza

1 quantity basic pizza dough
800 g/1 lb 12 oz canned
  chopped tomatoes
3–4 garlic cloves, finely chopped
1 tbsp dried oregano
55 g/2 oz capers

100 g/3½ oz black olives
200 g/7 oz Bel Paese cheese, grated
3 tbsp olive oil, plus extra
  for greasing
salt and pepper
flour, for dusting

Preheat the oven to 220°C/425°F/
Gas Mark 7 and grease four round
pizza tins.
    Divide the dough into four equal
portions and roll them into rounds
on a floured work surface. Place the
rounds on the prepared tins.

Distribute the tomatoes over the
dough. Season with the garlic,
oregano, and salt and pepper. Scatter
over the capers and olives and
sprinkle with the grated cheese.
Drizzle over the oil, then bake in the
preheated oven for about 20 minutes.

Pizza quattro stagioni
Four seasons pizza

1 quantity basic pizza dough
2 tbsp butter
200 g/7 oz mushrooms, sliced
6 tomatoes
200 g/7 oz cooked ham
200 g/7 oz mozzarella cheese
4 artichoke hearts in oil
16 stoned black olives
1 tsp dried oregano
3 tbsp olive oil, plus extra for greasing
salt and pepper
flour, for dusting

Preheat the oven to 220°C/425°F/Gas Mark 7 and grease four round pizza tins. Heat the butter in a frying pan, add the mushrooms and sauté for 10 minutes. Peel, quarter and deseed the tomatoes, then cut them into small dice. Cut the ham into small pieces. Thinly slice the cheese. Quarter the artichoke hearts.

Divide the dough into four equal portions and roll them out into rounds on a floured work surface. Place the rounds in the tins.

Distribute the tomatoes and cheese evenly between the pizzas. Cover one quarter of each pizza with one of the following toppings: mushrooms, ham, artichokes, olives. Season with the oregano and salt and pepper and drizzle over the oil. Bake in the preheated oven for about 20 minutes.

Pizza Margherita
Margherita Pizza

1 quantity basic pizza dough
90 ml/3 fl oz olive oil, plus extra
   for greasing
2 small onions, diced
400 g/14 oz canned diced tomatoes
500 g/1 lb 2 oz passata
1 tsp dried oregano
400 g/14 oz mozzarella cheese
salt and pepper
flour, for dusting
basil leaves, to garnish

Heat 4 tablespoons of the oil in a heavy-based saucepan, add the onions and sauté until translucent. Add the canned tomatoes, passata and oregano and season with salt and pepper. Cook the sauce for about 30 minutes over a medium heat.

Preheat the oven to 220°C/425°F/Gas Mark 7 and grease four round pizza tins. Divide the dough into four equal portions and roll them out into rounds on a floured work surface. Place the rounds in the tins.

Thinly slice the cheese. Brush the dough with the tomato sauce, lay the cheese slices on top and drizzle over the remaining oil. Bake in the preheated oven for about 20 minutes, then garnish with basil leaves and serve immediately.

Frittata con prezzemolo
Frittata with parsley

serves 4

6 eggs
1 bunch flat-leaf parsley,
    coarsely chopped
4 tbsp olive oil
salt and pepper

Beat the eggs in a bowl with some salt and pepper until foaming, then blend in the parsley.

Heat the olive oil in a heavy-based frying pan until it starts to smoke. Pour in the eggs and smooth the surface with a wooden spatula. Reduce the heat to low and allow the eggs to thicken.

As soon as the frittata begins to brown on the underside, use a plate to carefully turn over the frittata. Cook the other side until it is golden brown. Cut the frittata into 4 slices and serve while hot or warm.

Omelette agli spinaci e mozzarella
Spinach and mozzarella omelette

serves 4

1 tbsp butter
4 eggs, lightly beaten
40 g/1½ oz mozzarella cheese,
    thinly sliced and cut into
    bite-sized pieces
small handful baby spinach,
    stalks removed
salt and pepper
1 oil-cured red pepper,
    sliced into strips,
    to garnish

Heat a 25-cm/10-inch non-stick frying pan over a medium–high heat. Add the butter and, when it sizzles, pour in the eggs. Season with salt and pepper, then stir gently with the back of a fork until large flakes form. Leave to cook for a few seconds, then tilt the pan and lift the edges of the mixture with a spatula, so that the uncooked egg flows underneath.

Scatter the cheese and spinach over the top and leave to cook for a few seconds. Once the surface starts to solidify, carefully fold the omelette in half. Cook for a few seconds, pressing the surface with a spatula.

Turn over and cook for another few seconds, until the cheese is soft and the spinach wilted. Slip the omelette onto a warmed serving dish and slice into segments. Garnish with strips of red pepper before serving.

Mama's top ten tips for staying cheerful

1 Mama's philosophy is molto simple. Happy is as happy does. Cooking makes you happy? So cook. Reading makes you happy? Read. Football, opera, art make you happy? So play, sing, paint. Life is there to be enjoyed.

2 Spend some time outdoors every day. Feeling fresh air, sunshine, even rain on our faces reminds us we're alive — and that to be alive is the most wonderful thing of all.

3 Talk to children. The laughter of children is more intoxicating than wine.

4 Count your blessings. It's a cliché? The world was built on clichés! No matter how bad things seem, there are upsides — Mama's rule is that if you can think of enough to run out of fingers to count them on, you've enough good fortune to last the rest of your life.

5 Keep active. Stand still too long and you might begin to think it's not worth moving again.

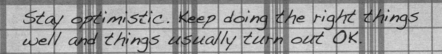

6 Stay optimistic. Keep doing the right things well and things usually turn out OK.

7 Keep your family close: and if you can't stay close physically then talk or write often. Two of my boys work far away in the city of Bari but Gianluca, the youngest, says that with his mobile telephone and something called email he can stay in touch every day: I have no idea what any of it really means but it sounds wonderful.

8 Close your eyes and eat a grape, an olive, some mozzarella cheese, a sundried tomato. Instant happiness!

9 Remember: life is not supposed to be easy... but it's not supposed to be miserable either. Misfortunes happen, sadness and grief follow us – but then so does incredible joy. So do laughter, love, beauty, warmth, comfort... even the simple pleasures of a good ciabatta and a toast of vino rosso with a man like Alberto can be enough to make up for whatever else the world throws at us.

10 A full belly makes a contented mind. Alberto is the happiest man I know: and he eats the best in all Italy.

Polpette di spinaci e ricotta
Spinach and ricotta patties

serves 4

450 g/1 lb fresh spinach
225 g/8 oz ricotta cheese
1 egg, beaten
2 tsp fennel seeds,
   lightly crushed
50 g/1¾ oz pecorino cheese or
   Parmesan cheese, finely
   grated, plus extra to garnish
25 g/1 oz plain flour,
   mixed with 1 tsp dried thyme
5 tbsp butter
2 garlic cloves, crushed
salt and pepper
tomato wedges, to serve

Wash the spinach and trim off any long stalks. Place in a large saucepan, cover and cook for 4—5 minutes, until wilted. This will probably have to be done in batches as the volume of spinach is quite large. Place in a colander to drain and cool.

Mash the ricotta cheese and beat in the egg and the fennel seeds. Season with plenty of salt and pepper, then stir in the pecorino cheese.

Squeeze as much excess water as possible from the spinach and finely chop the leaves. Stir the spinach into the cheese mixture. Take about 1 tablespoon of the spinach and cheese mixture, shape it into a ball and flatten it slightly to form a patty. Gently roll in the seasoned flour. Continue until all of the mixture has been used up.

Half-fill a large frying pan with water and bring to the boil. Carefully add the patties and cook for 3—4 minutes, or until they rise to the surface. Remove with a slotted spoon.

Melt the butter in a small saucepan. Add the garlic and cook for 2—3 minutes. Pour the garlic butter over the patties, season with pepper and serve at once with the tomato wedges, garnished and grated cheese.

Mozzarella in carrozza
Deep-fried mozzarella

serves 4

8 slices bread, preferably slightly stale, crusts removed
100 g/3½ oz mozzarella cheese, thickly sliced
55 g/2 oz black olives chopped
8 canned anchovy fillets, drained and chopped
16 fresh basil leaves, plus extra to garnish
4 eggs, beaten
150 ml/5 fl oz milk
salt and pepper
oil, for deep-frying

Cut each slice of bread into 2 triangles. Top 8 of the bread triangles with equal amounts of the cheese, olives and chopped anchovies. Place the basil leaves on top and season to taste with salt and pepper.

Lay the remaining 8 triangles of bread over the top and press down round the edges to seal.

Mix the eggs and milk together and pour into an ovenproof dish. Add the sandwiches and leave to soak for about 5 minutes.

Add oil to a large saucepan and heat to 180–190°C/350–375°F, or until a cube of bread browns in 30 seconds.

Before cooking the sandwiches, squeeze the edges together again. Carefully place the sandwiches in the oil and deep-fry for 2 minutes, or until golden, turning once. Remove the sandwiches with a slotted spoon and drain on kitchen paper. You will have to cook the sandwiches in batches.

Serve immediately while still hot.

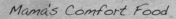

Patate e finocchio al forno
Potato and fennel bake

serves 6

1 kg/2 lb 4 oz potatoes
2–3 fennel bulbs
4 tbsp olive oil
1 onion, finely chopped
2 garlic cloves, crushed
4 fresh sage leaves
150 ml/5 fl oz dry white wine
salt and pepper

Preheat the oven to 200°C/400°F/Gas Mark 6. Peel, then finely slice the potatoes. Trim and finely slice the fennel.

Oil a large gratin dish with half the oil.

Layer half the potato slices in the base of the prepared dish and season well with salt and pepper. Sprinkle over half the onion and garlic and cover with the fennel. Sprinkle the remaining onion and garlic over and season again to taste with salt and pepper. Tuck the sage leaves into the vegetables. Finish with a neat layer of the potato slices and season again to taste with salt and pepper. Pour over the wine and drizzle over the remaining oil.

Cover the dish with foil and bake in the preheated oven for 30 minutes. Remove the foil and bake for a further 20—30 minutes, or until the potatoes are brown and crisp.

Mama's Tip

You can use a food processor fitted with a slicer attachment for slicing the potatoes, but a mandolin is the ideal tool to use.

Ravioli alla zucca
Pumpkin ravioli

serves 4

300 g/10½ oz durum wheat
   flour, plus extra for dusting
2 eggs
1 tbsp oil
½ tsp salt
1 tsp vinegar
3-4 tbsp water

filling
1 tbsp olive oil
450 g/1 lb pumpkin, cubed
1 shallot, finely diced
125 ml/4 fl oz water,
   plus extra for brushing
55 g/2 oz grated Parmesan cheese
1 egg
1 tbsp finely chopped fresh
   parsley
salt and pepper

Knead the flour, eggs, oil, salt, vinegar and water into a silky-smooth dough. Wrap the dough in clingfilm and chill in the refrigerator for 1 hour.

For the filling, heat the olive oil in a saucepan, add the pumpkin and shallot and sauté until the shallot is translucent. Add the water and cook the pumpkin until the liquid evaporates. Cool slightly, then mix with the cheese, egg, parsley, and salt and pepper.

Divide the dough in half. Thinly roll out both pieces. Place small spoonfuls of the pumpkin mixture about 4 cm/1½ inches apart on one sheet of dough. Brush a little water on the spaces in between. Lay the second sheet of dough on top and press down around each piece of filling. Use a pastry wheel to cut out squares and press the edges together with a fork.

Leave the ravioli to dry for 30 minutes, then bring a large saucepan of lightly salted water to the boil. Add the ravioli and cook over a medium heat until tender, but firm to the bite. Remove the ravioli with a slotted spoon and drain well on kitchen paper.

Ravioli al formaggio
Ravioli with feta cheese

300 g/10½ oz durum wheat flour,
    plus extra for dusting
2 eggs
1 tbsp oil
½ tsp salt
1 tsp vinegar
3-4 tbsp water

filling
250 g/9 oz feta cheese (drained weight)
2 garlic cloves, finely chopped
2 tbsp finely chopped fresh parsley
1 fresh red chilli,
    cored and finely chopped
salt and pepper

Knead the flour, eggs, oil, salt, vinegar and water
into a silky-smooth dough. Wrap the dough in clingfilm
and chill in the refrigerator for 1 hour.

For the filling, crumble the cheese and combine it
with the garlic, parsley and chilli. Season to taste
with salt and pepper.

Prepare the ravioli in the same way as for Pumpkin
ravioli (left).

Farfalle con pomodori secchi e basilico
· Farfalle with sun-dried tomatoes

serves 4

30 g/1 oz sun-dried tomatoes
55 g/2 oz pine kernels
1 handful fresh basil
2 garlic cloves, chopped
½ tsp salt
100 ml/3½ fl oz olive oil
1 tbsp grated Parmesan cheese
400 g/14 oz dried farfalle pasta
salt and pepper

Pour water over the sun-dried tomatoes and soak them for 25 minutes. Then pour off the water, squeeze out the liquid and chop.

Roast the pine kernels in a dry frying pan until golden brown. Grind half of the pine kernels with the basil leaves, garlic and salt in a large mortar. Gradually work in the olive oil. Add the cheese last.

Stir the chopped tomatoes into the basil sauce.

Bring a large saucepan of lightly salted water to the boil. Add the pasta and cook according to the instructions on the packet until tender, but still firm to the bite. Drain the pasta and combine it, still dripping wet, with the basil and tomato sauce in a warmed bowl. Serve on warmed plates, seasoned with pepper and sprinkled with the remaining pine kernels.

Cannelloni agli spinaci
Spinach cannelloni

serves 4

600 g/1 lb 5 oz spinach
1½ tbsp butter, plus extra
    for greasing
1 small onion, finely chopped
200 g/7 oz ricotta
    cheese
12 no-precook cannelloni tubes
600 ml/1 pint ready-prepared
    béchamel sauce
55 g/2 oz grated Parmesan cheese
grated nutmeg
salt and pepper

Preheat the oven to 200°C/400°F/Gas Mark 6 and grease a baking dish. Wash the spinach thoroughly and remove any wilted leaves and coarse stems. Heat the butter in a saucepan, add the onion and sauté until translucent.

Add the spinach while still dripping wet, cover the pan and allow the leaves to wilt. Drain the spinach well in a sieve, then chop it. Combine the spinach and ricotta cheese, then season with salt and pepper and nutmeg. Transfer the spinach mixture to a piping bag with a large nozzle and use it to fill the cannelloni tubes.

Lay the filled cannelloni side by side in the baking dish, cover with the béchamel sauce and sprinkle with the cheese. Bake in the preheated oven for 25—30 minutes.

Gnocchi alla Romana
Roman-style gnocchi

serves 4

475 ml/16 fl oz milk
400 ml/14 fl oz water
115 g/4 oz butter,
   plus extra for greasing
250 g/9 oz durum wheat semolina
100 g/3½ oz grated Parmesan
   cheese
2 egg yolks
grated nutmeg
2 tbsp grated fontina cheese
salt and pepper

Combine the milk, water, 2 tablespoons of butter and ½ teaspoon of salt in a large saucepan and bring to the boil. Gradually sprinkle in the semolina and cook over a low heat for 25—30 minutes, stirring constantly. Transfer the mixture to a bowl and stir in 2 tablespoons of the Parmesan cheese and the egg yolks. Season with salt and pepper and nutmeg. Set aside to cool.

Preheat the oven to 200°C/400°F/Gas Mark 6 and grease a baking dish. Use two spoons to form gnocchi from the semolina dough and set them in the baking dish. Mix the remaining Parmesan cheese with the fontina cheese and sprinkle over the gnocchi. Melt the remaining butter and pour it over the cheese. Bake the gnocchi in the preheated oven for about 20 minutes, until golden brown.

Quadrucci

Fettucine

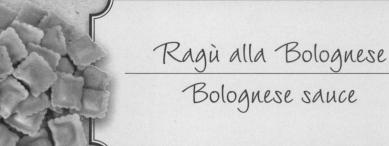

Ragù alla Bolognese
Bolognese sauce

serves 4

25 g/1 oz dried ceps
125 ml/4 fl oz lukewarm water
1 tbsp butter
55 g/2 oz pancetta, diced
1 small onion, finely chopped
1 garlic clove, finely chopped
2 small carrots, finely diced
2 celery sticks, finely diced
300 g/10½ oz beef mince
1 pinch sugar
freshly grated nutmeg
1 tbsp tomato purée
125 ml/4 fl oz red wine
250 g/9 oz passata
salt and pepper

Soak the ceps in the water for 20 minutes.

Melt the butter in a saucepan, add the pancetta and fry.

Add the onion and garlic and fry until the onion is translucent. Stir in the carrots and celery and cook for a few minutes, stirring frequently.

Add the beef and fry, stirring constantly. Season with salt and pepper, a pinch of sugar and some nutmeg. Stir in the tomato purée and cook for a minute or two, then add the wine. Mix in the passata. Thinly slice the ceps and add them to the sauce. Pour the soaking water through a fine sieve into the sauce. Thicken the sauce by cooking it over a low heat for 1 hour.

Tagliatelle

Spaghetti

Lasagne

Farfalle

Penne

Fusilli

Conchiglie

Cannelloni

Capelli d'Angelo

117

Spaghetti alla carbonara
Spaghetti carbonara

serves 4

400 g/14 oz dried spaghetti
4 eggs
4 tbsp double cream
55 g/2 oz grated Parmesan cheese
55 g/2 oz grated pecorino cheese
1 tbsp butter
150 g/5½ oz pancetta,
    finely diced
salt and pepper

Bring a large saucepan of lightly salted water to the boil. Add the spaghetti and cook according to the packet instructions or until tender, but firm to the bite.

Meanwhile, stir together the eggs, cream, Parmesan cheese and pecorino cheese in a bowl. Add salt and pepper.

Melt the butter in a large saucepan, add the pancetta, and fry until crispy. Drain the spaghetti and add it to the pan while still dripping wet. Pour the cheese sauce over it. Remove the pan from the heat. Toss the spaghetti in the sauce until the eggs begin to thicken but are still creamy.

Serve on warmed plates, sprinkled with pepper.

Lasagne al forno
Beef lasagne with ricotta and mozzarella

serves 6

175 ml/6 fl oz olive oil
55 g/2 oz butter
100 g/3½ oz pancetta
1 onion, finely chopped
1 celery stick, finely chopped
1 carrot, finely chopped
350 g/12 oz braising steak,
    in a single piece
5 tbsp red wine
2 tbsp sun-dried tomato purée
200 g/7 oz Italian sausage
2 eggs
150 g/5½ oz freshly grated
    Parmesan cheese
30 g/1 oz fresh breadcrumbs
350 g/12 oz ricotta cheese
8 dried no-precook lasagne sheets
350 g/12 oz mozzarella cheese,
    sliced
salt and pepper
chopped fresh parsley, to garnish

Heat 125 ml/4 fl oz of the oil with the butter in a large saucepan. Add the pancetta, onion, celery and carrot and cook over a low heat, until soft. Increase the heat to medium, add the steak and cook until evenly browned. Stir in the wine and tomato purée, season with salt and pepper and bring to the boil. Reduce the heat, cover and simmer gently for 1½ hours, until the steak is tender.

Meanwhile, heat 2 tablespoons of the remaining oil in a frying pan. Add the sausage and cook for 8—10 minutes. Remove from the pan and discard the skin. Thinly slice the sausage and set aside. Transfer the steak to a chopping board and finely dice. Return half the steak to the sauce.

Mix the remaining steak in a bowl with 1 egg, 1 tablespoon of the Parmesan cheese and the breadcrumbs. Shape into walnut-sized balls. Heat the remaining oil in a frying pan, add the meatballs and cook for 5—8 minutes, until brown. Pass the ricotta through a sieve into a bowl. Stir in the remaining egg and 4 tablespoons of the remaining Parmesan cheese.

Preheat the oven to 180°C/350°F/Gas Mark 4. In a rectangular ovenproof dish, make layers with the lasagne sheets, ricotta mixture, meat sauce, meatballs, sausage and mozzarella cheese. Finish with a layer of the ricotta mixture and sprinkle with the remaining Parmesan cheese.

Bake the lasagne in the preheated oven for 20—25 minutes, until cooked through and bubbling. Serve immediately, garnished with chopped parsley.

Fritto misto di mare
Lightly battered and fried fish

serves 4–6

18 large raw prawns
225 g/8 oz cleaned baby squid
6 red snapper fillets
light olive oil, for deep-frying
lemon wedges, to serve

batter
175 g/6 oz plain flour
2 eggs
225 ml/8 fl oz cold water
salt and pepper

To make the batter, sift the flour into a mixing bowl. Season the flour to taste with salt and pepper and make a well in the centre. Break the eggs into the well and add the water. Gradually beat the eggs and water into the flour to form a smooth batter.

Shell and devein the prawns. Cut the squid into tentacles and rings and cut the red snapper into small squares.

Heat the oil in a deep-fat fryer or a large heavy-based saucepan to 180°C/350°F, or until a cube of bread browns in 30 seconds. Dip the seafood in the batter and wipe off any excess. Add to the hot oil, in small batches, and cook for 2—3 minutes, or until crisp and golden. Remove with a slotted spoon, then drain on kitchen paper and keep warm while you cook the remaining seafood.

Pile onto warmed plates and season to taste with salt, then serve with lemon wedges.

Il cacciucco alla Livornese
Livorno seafood stew

Cut the red snapper fillets into thirds. Cut the monkfish into similar-sized pieces, cutting the flesh away from the tailbone (this can be used to make stock). Cut the squid into thick rings and retain the tentacles. Heat the oil in a large saucepan, then add the onion, garlic and fennel and cook over a medium heat, stirring frequently, for 4—5 minutes, or until starting to soften. Pour in the wine and stir well, then leave to bubble until almost evaporated. Add the tomatoes and bring to the boil, then reduce the heat and simmer, uncovered, for 10—15 minutes, or until the fennel is tender and the sauce is reduced and thickened.

serves 6

4 red snapper fillets
450 g/1 lb monkfish tail
400 g/14 oz cleaned baby squid
3 tbsp olive oil
1 onion, finely chopped
2 garlic cloves, finely chopped
2 fennel bulbs, finely sliced
150 ml/5 fl oz dry white wine
600 g/1 lb 5 oz canned chopped tomatoes
750 ml/1¼ pints fish stock
500 g/1 lb 2 oz live mussels, scrubbed and debearded
18 large raw prawns, shelled and deveined
salt and pepper

To serve
2 tbsp finely chopped fresh flat-leaf parsley
6 slices ciabatta bread, toasted, rubbed with garlic, and drizzled with olive oil

Meanwhile, bring the stock to the boil in a separate large saucepan, then add the mussels and cook, covered, over a high heat for 3—4 minutes, shaking the pan occasionally, until the mussels have opened. Discard any that remain closed. Strain the mussels, reserving the stock. Remove half the mussels from their shells, discarding the shells. Keep all the mussels warm. Add the reserved stock to the tomato mixture and bring to the boil. Add the snapper, monkfish, squid and prawns to the pan and cook for 2—3 minutes, or until tender and the prawns have turned pink. Add the shelled and unshelled mussels and heat through. Season to taste with salt and pepper.

Divide evenly between individual warmed soup dishes and sprinkle with parsley. Serve each dish with the toasted bread slices.

Mama's tips for taking it easy

Good cooking can't be rushed: bread needs time to rise, flavours need space to infuse properly. Standing over the cooker worrying will not make things happen any quicker. Learn to love the wait: it's where the magic happens!

In Italy we say that 'La calma è la virtù dei forti' — calm is the virtue of the strong. Nowhere is this more true than in Mama's kitchen...

Slow down. Why is the younger generation always in such a hurry? My children's children, my nipoti, are forever rushing to do everything at once: they're so intent on getting where they're going, they're not enjoying the journey. Like Alberto says — when you try to see everything, you see nothing.

Don't worry about perfection. Roma wasn't built in a day — and even when it was built, it wasn't built perfectly.

Mistakes happen, in cookery and in life. Bread burns, meat spoils, sauces separate... 'Così va il mondo' — so the world goes. Tomorrow we'll be cooking again.

Change is inevitable... but tradition is what gives us our identity and our strength. The old ways of doing things are often the old ways because they're the best ways. And never more so than in the kitchen. Think of the wooden spoon: a thousand years of progress has not improved on that most simple design.

The key to an easy life is flexibility — be the Italian olive tree that bends in the wind and not the English oak that snaps.

Most important of all: listen to your mama. Because you're not only listening to her wisdom, but the wisdom of her mama... and her mama before her. If everyone listened to their mamas, the world would be a much happier, more relaxed place.

Zabaione
Zabaglione

serves 6

75 g/2¾ oz caster sugar
6 egg yolks
175 ml/6 fl oz Marsala, Madeira
or other sweet dessert wine
splash of brandy
amaretto biscuits, to serve

Fill a saucepan halfway with water and bring to the boil. Place a heatproof bowl over the pan so that it doesn't quite touch the boiling water.

Put the sugar and eggs into the bowl and whisk until light and creamy. Add the Marsala a little at a time, whisking constantly, then add the brandy and continue whisking for up to 15 minutes, until you have a floaty, silky foam.

Pour it into bowls and serve with amaretto biscuits. It can also be made ahead of time and served chilled.

Dolce di panettone
Panettone bread-and-butter pudding

serves 4–6

100 g/3½ oz raisins, sultanas
  or chopped dates
4 tbsp brandy
300 ml/10 fl oz milk
450 ml/16 fl oz double cream
1 vanilla pod, split, or 1 tsp
  vanilla extract
175 g/6 oz butter, softened,
  plus extra for greasing
10 medium loaf-sized slices of
  panettone, preferably
  chocolate-flavoured, or white
  bread, crusts removed
4 eggs
175 g/6 oz caster sugar
vanilla ice cream, to serve

Put the raisins in a bowl with the brandy and leave to soften for an hour or two. In a small saucepan, warm (but don't boil) the milk and cream and add the split vanilla pod. Leave to stand for 30 minutes.

Preheat the oven to 180°C/350°F/Gas Mark 4. Butter a shallow ovenproof dish. Butter the panettone slices, cut them diagonally in half and lay in an overlapping pattern in the dish. Remove the softened raisins from the brandy, reserving the brandy, and sprinkle them over the panettone.

In a large bowl, whisk the eggs with the sugar. Remove the vanilla pod from the milk and discard, then add the milk and cream to the egg mixture. Add the reserved brandy and whisk.

Pour this mixture over the panettone and press the slices down so that they soak in the custard. Make sure that the edges don't stick out too far above the surface of the custard. Transfer to the preheated oven and bake for 30–40 minutes, until the custard has dried and set golden brown, but before the panettone burns. Serve hot, with vanilla ice cream.

Tiramisù
Tiramisù

serves 4

3 egg yolks
4 tbsp amaretto
175 g/6 oz caster sugar
50 g/1¾ oz plain chocolate,
    finely grated
150 g/5½ oz mascarpone
    cheese
175 ml/6 fl oz double cream
24 ladyfingers
espresso
200 g/7 oz cocoa powder,
    for dusting

Whisk together the egg yolks and amaretto. Gradually add the sugar and beat until the sugar has dissolved completely. Stir in the chocolate and mascarpone cheese.

Whip the cream and fold it in.

Dip the unsugared side of each ladyfinger into the espresso. Arrange half the ladyfingers on the bottom of a square or rectangular dish, then cover with half the mascarpone cream.

Layer the remaining ladyfingers and cream, spreading it evenly. Cover the dish and chill overnight in the refrigerator.

Before serving, dust heavily with cocoa.

My dearest Luisa, it was so nice to spend time with you and Gianluca and the bambini, relaxing under the shade of the trees, enjoying the delicious food that is so abundant in our wonderful Apulian summer. . . . washed down, of course, with some of our excellent Apulian vino!

MOINEAU-PIERROT

Mama's Day Out!

Who says Mama's place is in the kitchen? Well, Alberto some days, but forget him for the moment — because when the summer sun is warm on the hills and Mama has a new hat to wear, nothing is better than a picnic!

Preparing food for a day out should not just mean the same old sandwiches. The following pages are full to bursting with bright, imaginative, mouthwatering ideas for the hamper: whether it's olives with oranges and lemon, broad bean and pecorino salad, tomato tart or dozens of other quick and easy recipes, putting on a spread all'aperto will never have been so simple — or tasted so good.

Funghi sott'olio
Mushrooms preserved in oil

serves 4

1 kg/2 lb 4 oz small mushrooms
(button mushrooms, ceps,
chanterelles, honey mushrooms)
1 fresh red chilli
225 ml/8 fl.oz olive oil
125 ml/4 fl oz white balsamic
vinegar
1 small sprig oregano or
rosemary

salt

Clean the mushrooms and pat dry with kitchen paper.

Cut the chilli in half, remove the core and cut the flesh into fine strips.

Heat 5 tablespoons of the oil in a large frying pan, add the mushrooms and brown on all sides until the liquid has evaporated.

Add the chilli to the pan and sauté briefly. Deglaze the pan with the vinegar, add salt, then transfer the mushrooms to a bowl. Add the oregano and the remaining oil. Cover and leave the mushrooms to marinate overnight.

Red chilli pepper

Ceps

Verdure miste sott'olio
Mixed vegetables in oil

serves 4

2 aubergines
2 large courgettes
200 g/7 oz oyster mushrooms
225 ml/8 fl oz olive oil,
   plus extra for greasing
2 garlic cloves, thinly sliced
leaves of 4–5 thyme sprigs
2 bay leaves
125 ml/4 fl oz red wine vinegar
salt and pepper

Trim the aubergines and courgettes and cut into slices. Clean the mushrooms and cut into halves or quarters, depending on their size. Coat a grill pan with oil and grill the vegetables in portions for 2–3 minutes on each side. Place the grilled slices in a bowl and add salt and pepper.

Sprinkle the garlic and thyme leaves over the vegetables, and place the bay leaves in between them.

Whisk the oil, vinegar, and salt and pepper together and pour over the warm vegetables.

Leave to cool, then cover with clingfilm and chill overnight in the refrigerator. Remove the vegetables from the refrigerator 30 minutes before serving.

Olive con arancio e limone
Olives with orange and lemon

serves 4

2 tsp fennel seeds
2 tsp cumin seeds
300 g/10½ oz green olives
300 g/10½ oz black olives
2 tsp grated orange rind
2 tsp grated lemon rind
3 shallots, finely chopped
pinch of ground cinnamon
50 ml/2 fl oz white wine vinegar
50 ml/2 fl oz extra virgin
   olive oil
2 tbsp orange juice
1 tbsp chopped fresh mint
1 tbsp chopped fresh parsley

Dry-roast the fennel seeds and cumin seeds in a small, heavy-based frying pan, shaking the pan frequently, until they begin to pop and give off their aroma. Remove the pan from the heat and leave to cool.

Place the olives, orange rind, lemon rind, shallots, cinnamon and roasted seeds in a bowl.

Whisk the vinegar, oil, orange juice, mint and parsley together in a bowl and pour over the olives. Toss well, then cover and leave to chill for 1—2 days before serving.

Mama's essential picnic equipment

A beautiful summer day, birds soaring in the air, flowers nodding in the sunshine, the merry buzz of bees around and adults and children eating all'aperto... what in all the world could be better than a picnic?

• Planning a picnic is about so much more than deciding what food to take. Bear in mind that once you've arrived, there can be no popping back for anything you've forgotten. Write a list and keep it to use every summer.

• If you pack everything up to eat in the countryside as often as Mama and Alberto do, a good hamper is a necessity. Wicker is strong and light and looks the part too — but whichever you get, make sure it has straps to secure the plates, cups and cutlery as well as the food.

An old jar with some honey in it is the best way of keeping wasps away from the party. Place it a short distance away and they should leave you to enjoy your food in peace.

A picnic without wine is no picnic at all. Don't forget the corkscrew!

Even in the gentle Apulian countryside, sitting on the grass for too long has its drawbacks. Take plenty of rugs to spread out – some for food, some for people. And for those with creaking limbs like Mama, folding chairs are necessary too!

If you can afford (and can carry) a lightweight gazebo, they can make the difference between an ordinary lunch in the country and the kind of picnic you'll wish could last all weekend. As well as providing shade from the sun and shelter from the wind, they're a natural place for entertaining the children.

Pomodori ripiene di tonno
Tuna-stuffed tomatoes

serves 4

4 large, firm beef tomatoes
150 g/5½ oz canned tuna in oil
2 hard-boiled eggs
1 small onion, finely chopped
4 tbsp mayonnaise
1 tbsp finely chopped fresh
   parsley
salt and pepper
4 lettuce leaves

Wash the tomatoes and cut off the tops, including the stems, for use as lids. Scoop out the core and seeds with a spoon.

Salt the insides of the tomatoes, place upside down in a sieve and leave to drain.

Drain the tuna and flake it with a fork. Peel and chop the eggs. Combine the onion, tuna and egg with the mayonnaise and parsley, then add salt and pepper to taste.

Put the filling in the tomatoes, set the tops back on and arrange the filled tomatoes on the lettuce leaves.

Tramezzini al prosciutto e rucola
Ham and rocket sandwiches

makes 4
8 slices sandwich bread
2 tbsp mayonnaise
2 handfuls rocket
150 g/5½ oz cooked ham,
    sliced
2 tomatoes, sliced
a few basil leaves
salt and pepper

Remove the crusts from the bread and spread mayonnaise on each slice. Place rocket on 4 slices, then layer with ham and tomatoes. Season with salt and pepper.

Divide the basil leaves between the sandwiches and top with the remaining bread slices. Slice each sandwich diagonally.

Prosciutto, mortadella or sliced mozzarella cheese can be substituted for the ham.

Tramezzini al tonno
Tuna sandwiches

makes 4
200 g/7 oz canned tuna
    in oil, drained
1 tbsp capers
2 hard-boiled eggs
8 slices sandwich bread
3-4 tbsp black olive paste
8 lettuce leaves

Flake the tuna with a fork.
Finely chop the capers and
combine them with the tuna.
Peel the eggs and slice evenly.
    Cut the crusts off the bread
and spread each slice with a
little of the olive paste.
    Divide the tuna-caper mixture
between 4 slices of bread.
Top these with sliced egg and
2 lettuce leaves, then cover with
the remaining slices of bread.
Cut each sandwich diagonally.

Tramezzini ai gamberi
Prawn sandwiches

makes 4
175 g/6 oz small prawns,
    cooked and shelled
1 tbsp lime juice
2 hard-boiled eggs
4 tbsp mayonnaise
8 slices sandwich bread
4 lettuce leaves
salt and pepper

Season the prawns with the lime
juice and salt and pepper. Peel
and chop the eggs. Mix the prawns
with the eggs and 2 tablespoons
of mayonnaise.
    Remove the bread crusts and
spread the rest of the mayonnaise
on 4 slices.
    Spread the prawn mixture on
the remaining slices and top each
one with a lettuce leaf. Cover
with the mayonnaise-spread bread
slices and cut each sandwich
diagonally.

Involtini di asparagi e prosciutto
Asparagus and prosciutto wraps

serves 6

225 g/8 oz asparagus, trimmed
375-g/13-oz pack ready-rolled
  chilled puff pastry sheet
  (35 x 23 cm/14 x 9 inches)
2 tbsp pesto
6 thin slices prosciutto
85 g/3 oz grated Emmenthal cheese
milk, for brushing
pepper

Preheat the oven to 220°C/425°F/Gas Mark 7.

Bring a large saucepan of water to the boil, add the asparagus, cook for 5—6 minutes, until tender, and drain.

Cut the pastry into six 12-cm/4½-inch squares. Place on a baking sheet and spread 1 teaspoon of pesto on the centre of each.

Divide the asparagus into 6 bunches and wrap each in a slice of prosciutto. Place diagonally on each square of pastry and top with grated cheese and pepper.

Lift the opposite corners of the pastry to meet on top, brushing with milk to glaze. Bake in the preheated oven for 15—20 minutes, until golden. Serve the wraps warm or cold, lunchtime or picnic treat.

Fichi e Gorgonzola
Figs with Gorgonzola

serves 4

70 g/2½ oz caster sugar
85 g/3 oz whole almonds,
   blanched or unblanched
12 ripe figs
350 g/12 oz Gorgonzola cheese,
   cubed
butter, for greasing
extra virgin olive oil,
   for drizzling

Lightly grease a baking sheet with butter. Put the sugar in a saucepan over a medium—high heat and stir until the sugar melts and turns golden brown and bubbles; do not stir once the mixture starts to bubble. Remove from the heat and add the almonds one at a time, quickly turning with a fork until coated; if the caramel begins to harden, return the pan to the heat. Transfer each coated almond to the prepared baking sheet.

Leave to cool until firm. To serve, slice the figs into quarters and arrange 8 quarters on each plate. Coarsely chop the almonds by hand. Place a mound of cheese on each plate and sprinkle with chopped almonds. Drizzle the figs very lightly with oil.

Insalata di fave e pecorino
Broad bean and pecorino salad

serves 6

225 g/8 oz shelled fresh
   broad beans
5 tbsp extra virgin olive oil
2 tbsp freshly squeezed lemon
   juice
1 tbsp chopped fresh mint
175 g/6 oz young pecorino
   cheese, cut into cubes
90 g/3¼ oz rocket
55 g/2 oz aged pecorino cheese
   or Parmesan cheese, shaved
salt and pepper

If the beans are extremely fresh and tiny, you can serve them raw, but otherwise blanch them for 2—3 minutes in a large saucepan of boiling water. Drain, then rinse under cold running water and drain again.

Put the drained beans in a dish. Pour over the oil and lemon juice, then add the mint. Season well with salt and pepper and mix in the cheese cubes.

Arrange the rocket on a serving dish and spoon over the bean and cheese mixture. Sprinkle over the cheese shavings and serve.

Mama's Tip
If you use older beans or frozen ones, you will need 50 per cent more beans to allow for the removal of the skins.

Bruschette con mozzarella
Bruschetta with mozzarella

serves 4

4 slices Tuscan country bread
2 garlic cloves
4 tbsp olive oil
150 g/5½ oz buffalo
   mozzarella cheese, sliced
2 tomatoes, sliced
salt and pepper
fresh basil leaves, to garnish

Toast the bread slices on both sides, either under a grill or in the oven, until golden brown.

Cut the garlic cloves in half. Rub each slice of bread with the cut side of a halved garlic clove, drizzle with 1 tablespoon of olive oil, then cut in half. Top the bread with sliced cheese, tomatoes, and salt and pepper, and garnish with basil leaves.

Toast al formaggio e pomodori secchi
Cheese and sun-dried tomato toasts

serves 4

4 slices Tuscan country bread
175 g/6 oz sun-dried tomato purée
300 g/10½ oz mozzarella cheese,
    drained and diced
1¼ tsp dried oregano
2-3 tbsp olive oil
pepper

Preheat the oven to 220°C/425°F/Gas Mark 7. Toast the slices on both sides under a preheated grill until golden.

Spread one side of each toast with the sun-dried tomato purée and top with cheese. Sprinkle with oregano and season to taste with pepper.

Place the toasts on a large baking sheet and drizzle with olive oil. Bake in the preheated oven for about 5 minutes, until the cheese has melted and is bubbling. Remove the hot toasts from the oven and leave to stand for 5 minutes before serving.

Sgonfiotti al formaggio
Fried cheese pastries

makes about 25

200 g/7 oz plain flour,
  plus extra for dusting
2 eggs, lightly beaten
2 tbsp olive oil
1-2 tbsp cold water
1 egg white, beaten until
  slightly frothy
salt
vegetable oil, for deep-frying

filling
115 g/4 oz ricotta cheese
1 egg, lightly beaten
70 g/2½ oz mozzarella cheese,
  finely diced
25 g/1 oz Parmesan cheese,
  finely diced
40 g/1½ oz salami or Parma ham,
  finely chopped
1 tbsp chopped fresh flat-leaf
  parsley
salt and pepper

To make the filling, mix all the ingredients together in a bowl and season to taste. Sift the flour into a large bowl. Make a well in the centre and pour in the eggs. Add the oil and a pinch of salt. Stir with a fork, gradually drawing in the flour from around the edge. Once a dough has formed, knead for about 10 minutes, until smooth and silky. Wrap the dough in clingfilm and leave to rest in the refrigerator for at least 30 minutes or overnight.

Roll out the dough very thinly and, using a pastry cutter, cut out rounds about 7 cm/2¾ inches in diameter, re-rolling the dough until it is all used. Place the rounds on a clean tea towel. Wet the edges of the rounds with egg white. Place a teaspoon of filling in the middle, then fold over one half of the dough to form a semi-circle. Press the edges together, making sure they stick. Leave to rest on the tea towel for 30 minutes.

Heat the oil in a deep-fat fryer or large saucepan to 180°C/350°C, or until a cube of bread browns in 30 seconds. Drop the pastries into the hot oil, a few at a time, deep-frying for 3—5 minutes. Remove from the pan and drain on crumpled kitchen paper. Serve at once, while still hot.

Torta di pomodori
Tomato tart

serves 4

2 tbsp butter
1 tbsp caster sugar
500 g/1 lb 2 oz cherry tomatoes,
   halved
1 clove garlic, crushed
2 tsp white wine vinegar
salt and pepper
chopped fresh oregano, to garnish

pastry
250 g/9 oz plain flour
pinch of salt
1 tbsp chopped tomatoes
140 g/5 oz butter
5-6 tbsp cold water

Preheat the oven to 200°C/400°F/Gas Mark 6. Melt the butter in a heavy-based saucepan. Add the sugar and stir over a fairly high heat until just turning golden brown.

Remove from the heat and quickly add the tomatoes, garlic and vinegar, stirring to coat evenly. Season with salt and pepper.

Tip the tomatoes into a 23-cm/9-inch round cake tin, spreading evenly.

For the pastry, place the flour, salt, tomatoes and butter in a food processor and process to fine crumbs. Add just enough water to bind to a soft, but not sticky, dough.

Roll out to a 25-cm/10-inch round and place over the tomatoes, tucking in the edges. Pierce with a fork to release the steam.

Bake in the preheated oven for 25—30 minutes, until firm and golden. Leave to rest for 2—3 minutes, then run a knife around the edge and turn out onto a warmed plate. Garnish with oregano and serve.

Mama's Tip
Serve the tart warm,
sprinkled with chopped
oregano, with a rocket
or baby spinach salad.

Crostini
Topped toasts

Crostini neri
Crostini with olive paste

serves 4

200 g/7 oz black olives,
   stoned
3 anchovy fillets in oil
1 tbsp capers
3-4 tbsp olive oil
12 small slices Tuscan
   white bread or ciabatta
12 basil leaves
salt
cayenne pepper

Coarsely chop the olives
and anchovy fillets, then
purée them together with
the capers and as much oil
as is needed to make a thick
paste. Season to taste with
salt and cayenne pepper.
   Toast the bread on both
sides under a grill or
in the oven until golden
brown.
   Spread each slice with
olive paste and garnish
with a basil leaf.

Crostini con erbe e pomodori
**Crostini with herbs and
   tomatoes**

serves 4

6 plum tomatoes
1 small bunch basil
2 garlic cloves, finely
   chopped
3 tbsp olive oil
1 tbsp finely chopped
   fresh parsley
½ tsp finely chopped fresh
   oregano
12 small slices Tuscan
   white bread or ciabatta
salt and pepper

Peel the tomatoes, quarter,
core and cut into small
cubes. Cut the basil leaves
into fine strips. Combine
the tomatoes with the
garlic, oil, salt and pepper
and herbs and leave to stand
briefly.
   Toast the bread on both
sides under a grill or in
the oven until golden brown.
   Spread each slice with
some of the tomato mixture.

Crostini alla Toscana
**Crostini with chicken
   liver pâté**

serves 4

200 g/7 oz chicken livers
2 tbsp olive oil
1 shallot, finely chopped
125 ml/4 fl oz Vin Santo
1 tbsp finely chopped
   fresh thyme
12 small slices of Tuscan
   white bread or ciabatta
salt and pepper

Rinse and dry the chicken
livers, remove the membranes,
then chop into small pieces.
   Heat the oil in a large
frying pan, add the shallot,
and sauté until translucent.
Add the livers and sauté.
Deglaze the pan with the
wine, add the thyme and
cook until the wine has
almost evaporated. Remove
from the heat, leave to cool
slightly, then purée. Season
with salt and pepper.
   Toast the bread on both
sides under a grill or in
the oven until golden brown.
Leave to cool slightly, then
spread with the pâté and
serve immediately.

Crostini al pomodoro
Crostini with tomatoes

serves 4

12 small slices Tuscan
  white bread or ciabatta
2 garlic cloves
2-3 tbsp olive oil
4 small beef tomatoes,
  sliced
50 g/1¾ oz Parmesan cheese
salt and pepper
a few basil leaves,
  to garnish

Toast the bread on both
sides under a grill or in
the oven until golden brown.
Peel the garlic cloves and
cut them in half. Rub the
toasted bread with garlic
and drizzle with oil. Top
with tomato slices, season
with salt and pepper and
thinly grate the cheese over
the tomatoes.

   Cut the basil into fine
strips and garnish the
toasts with them.

Prosciutto con la rucola
Prosciutto with rocket

serves 4

115 g/4 oz rocket
1 tbsp lemon juice
3 tbsp extra virgin olive oil
225 g/8 oz prosciutto, sliced
    thinly
salt and pepper

Place the rocket in a bowl.

Pour the lemon juice into a small bowl and season to taste with salt and pepper. Whisk in the olive oil, then pour the dressing over the rocket leaves and toss lightly so they are evenly coated.

Carefully drape the prosciutto in folds on 4 individual serving plates, then add the rocket and serve at room temperature.

Risi e bisi
Rice and peas

serves 4

1 litre/1¾ pints chicken stock,
   or vegetable stock
6 tbsp butter
3 shallots, finely chopped
115 g/4 oz pancetta or rindless
   lean bacon, diced
225 g/8 oz rice
150 ml/5 fl oz dry white wine
175 g/6 oz petits pois,
   thawed, if frozen
salt and pepper
Parmesan cheese shavings,
   to garnish

Pour the stock into a large saucepan and bring to the boil. Reduce the heat and leave to simmer gently.

Melt 4 tablespoons of the butter in a large, heavy-based saucepan. Add the shallots and pancetta and cook over a low heat, stirring occasionally, for 5 minutes, until the shallots are soft. Add the rice and cook, stirring constantly, for 2—3 minutes, until all the grains are thoroughly coated and glistening.

Pour in the wine and cook, stirring constantly, until it has almost completely evaporated. Add a ladleful of hot stock and cook, stirring constantly, until all the stock has been absorbed. Continue cooking and adding the stock, a ladleful at a time, for about 10 minutes.

Add the peas, then continue adding the stock, a ladleful at a time, for a further 10 minutes, or until the rice is tender and the liquid has been absorbed.

Stir in the remaining butter and season to taste with salt and pepper.

Transfer to a warmed serving dish, garnish with cheese shavings and serve

immediately.

Mama's tips on keeping the kids entertained

Every year all Mama's family get together for a picnic: at the last count there were 38 of us, aged from six months to more than 80 years! Making sure that there is enough food for everyone is hard work. Such a day out also means a lot of preparation has to go in to keeping the little ones happy...

In Apulia we say, 'Nelle botti piccine ci sta il vino buono': you find the good wine in the small barrels. Children bring joy to any occasion — they should not be sidelined to fit in with the adults' plans, but celebrated as the centre around which the whole day out revolves.

Children never stop running. Use that energy to let them work up an appetite: frisbees, footballs and tennis rackets are all essential. Last summer my sons Marco and Filippo organized all the children into teams for a game they made up as they went along, like a cross between touch rugby and American football, played with a frisbee. It was a great success... and if they can remember the rules it's sure to be played again this year.

Of course, there is one sure way to keep any child entertained: good food and plenty of it!

For those who are too little to join in the sport, a sing-song and even a dance will help keep them happy.

My daughter Maria's husband always brings fishing rods for the bigger children and nets for the little ones. Every year they swear they'll catch something for supper — and every year Mama has to inspect the tiddlers in the jam jars, consider carefully, and announce that if we put them back, then maybe they'll be big enough to eat next year...

Don't forget the old games. Mama used to play hide-and-seek in the olive groves here back before the war — and I still smile when I see the children today running to hide in the same places I did as a little girl.

Biscotti/cantucci di mandorle
Almond biscuits

makes 20-30

200 g/7 oz whole blanched almonds
200 g/7 oz plain flour,
   plus 1 tbsp for dusting
200 g/7 oz caster sugar,
   plus 1 tbsp for sprinkling
1 tsp baking powder
½ tsp ground cinnamon
2 eggs
2 tsp vanilla extract

Preheat the oven to 180°C/350°F/Gas Mark 4. Line two baking sheets with baking paper.

Very coarsely chop the almonds, leaving some whole.

Mix the flour, sugar, baking powder and cinnamon together in a mixing bowl. Stir in all the almonds.

Beat the eggs with the vanilla extract in a small bowl, then add to the flour mixture and mix together to form a firm dough.

Turn out the dough onto a lightly floured work surface and knead lightly. Divide the dough in half and shape each piece into a long, thick log, roughly 5 cm/2 inches wide. Transfer to the prepared baking sheets and sprinkle with sugar, then bake in the preheated oven for 20–25 minutes, or until brown and firm. Remove from the oven and leave to cool for a few minutes, then transfer the logs to a chopping board and cut into 1-cm/1/2-inch slices. Meanwhile, reduce the oven temperature to 160°C/325°F/Gas Mark 3. Arrange the biscuits, cut-side down, on the baking sheets. Bake in the oven for 15–20 minutes, or until dry and crisp. Remove from the oven and leave to cool on a wire rack. Store in an airtight container to keep crisp.

Mama's Tip
Almonds are traditional,
but you can make these
biscuits with any other
nuts, such as walnuts
or pistachio nuts.

Torta al cioccolato
Soft chocolate cake

serves 6-8

280 g/10 oz plain chocolate with at least 72% cocoa solids, broken into pieces
125 g/4½ oz unsalted butter, plus extra for greasing
4 eggs, separated
55 g/2 oz caster sugar
25 g/1 oz plain flour
1 tsp vanilla extract
cocoa powder, for dusting

Preheat the oven to 180°C/350°F/Gas Mark 4. Grease and base-line a 20-cm/8-inch springform cake tin with a removable base. Put the chocolate and butter in a heatproof bowl, then set the bowl over a saucepan of barely simmering water and heat until melted. Remove the bowl from the heat and leave to cool for 5 minutes.

Whisk the egg yolks and sugar together in a mixing bowl with a hand-held electric mixer or a hand whisk until thick and creamy. In a separate mixing bowl, whisk the egg whites until thick and glossy. Fold the egg yolk mixture into the melted chocolate.

Sift the flour and fold in together with the vanilla extract. Gently fold in the beaten egg whites.

Turn the mixture into the prepared tin and bake in the preheated oven for 15–20 minutes. Do not overcook. The top should be firm but the centre still slightly gooey. Remove from the oven and leave to cool, covered, overnight.

Remove the cake tin and peel away the lining paper from the base. Dust the surface of the cake with cocoa and serve in slices.

Cenci
Deep-fried pastry ribbons

serves 8

280 g/10 oz plain flour,
   plus extra for dusting
2 eggs, beaten
2 tbsp light olive oil
2 tbsp caster sugar
2 tbsp Vin Santo
finely grated rind of 1 lemon
4 oranges
sunflower oil, for deep-frying
icing sugar, for dusting

Sift the flour into a large mixing bowl and make a well in the centre. Add the eggs, the olive oil, sugar, Vin Santo and lemon rind. Mix together with a round-bladed knife to form a dough. Use your hands to knead until smooth. Form into a ball, then wrap in clingfilm and chill in the refrigerator for 1 hour.

Meanwhile, working over a bowl to catch the juice, peel and segment the oranges with a sharp knife. Add the segments to the juice, then cover and chill in the refrigerator until required.

Divide the dough in half and roll out one half on a lightly floured work surface to a rectangle about 3 mm/⅛ inch thick. Cover and repeat with the remaining dough. Using a fluted pastry cutting wheel, cut the dough into 10 x 2.5-cm/4 x 1-inch ribbons. Tie a single knot in each ribbon. Alternatively, cut the dough into diamond shapes and leave flat.

Heat the oil for deep-frying in a deep-fat fryer or a deep, heavy-based saucepan to 180°C/350°F, or until a cube of bread browns in 30 seconds. Add the ribbons, in small batches, and cook until golden brown. Remove with a slotted spoon and drain on kitchen paper, then keep warm while you cook the remaining ribbons. Dust with icing sugar before serving warm, with the orange segments.

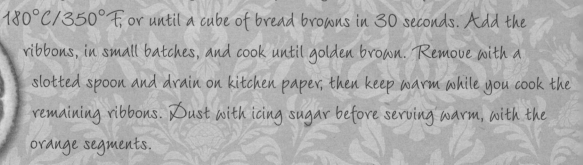

Mama's Tip
Sliced ripe apricots
and peaches could be
used instead of oranges.
Marinate in 3 tablespoons
of Vin Santo.

My dear Luisa, I am so pleased to hear you had success with the ciabatta recipe!

Mama's Baking Day

Where would we be without baking? Everyone knows Italians make the best bread in the world, and everyone in this part of Apulia knows Mama makes the best in Italy. Included here are no less than seven bread recipes, including ciabatta, focaccia with sage and a pesto and olive soda bread that Alberto swears tastes better than anything in all of Italy.

As if that wasn't enough, there are galette, pastries, tarts, pies, Stromboli... and even brioche, and Mama's favourite bad habit: biscotti.

Baking need not be as *difficile* as they say: follow Mama's advice and baking day will be a day of both comfort and self-indulgence.

Pane casalingo di oliva
Homemade olive bread

makes 3 small loaves

500 g/1 lb 2oz strong white
    flour, plus extra for dusting
1 sachet easy-blend dried yeast
1 tsp salt
1 pinch sugar
300 ml/10 fl oz lukewarm water
250 g/9 oz Swiss chard,
    chopped
100 g/3½ oz black olives,
    stoned and chopped
2 tbsp olive oil,
    plus extra for greasing

Sift the flour into a bowl and make a hollow in the middle. Place the yeast, salt and sugar in the hollow, then add the water. Knead the mixture into a smooth, silky dough. Leave it to rise, covered, for about 1 hour, or until doubled in size.

Preheat the oven to 220°C/425°F/Gas Mark 7 and grease a baking sheet. Knead the Swiss chard and olives into the dough, then divide it into thirds.

Form each third into a rounded rectangular loaf and place on the greased baking sheet. Cover with a flour-dusted tea towel and leave to rise again for 1 hour.

Brush the loaves with oil and bake in the preheated oven for 20—25 minutes. Leave to cool thoroughly on a wire rack.

Focaccia con cipolle
Flatbread with onions

makes 1 loaf

2 sachets easy-blend dried yeast
225 ml/8 fl oz lukewarm water
pinch of sugar
450 g/1 lb strong white flour,
    plus extra for dusting
1 tsp salt
125 ml/4 fl oz olive oil,
    plus extra for greasing
2 onions, cut into thin rings
100 g/3½ oz black olives, stoned
2–3 garlic cloves, finely chopped
1 tbsp coarse sea salt
2 tsp crushed peppercorns

Crumble the yeast into the lukewarm water, add the sugar and dissolve.

Stir in 4 tablespoons of the flour, cover and leave the resulting dough to prove in a warm place for 15 minutes.

Sift the remaining flour into a bowl, make a hollow in the centre and pour the dough into it. Add the salt and 3—4 tablespoons of oil and knead into a silky dough. Shape it into a ball, cover and set aside in a warm place to rise for 1 hour, or until doubled in volume.

Grease a baking sheet with oil and preheat the oven to 240°C/475°F/Gas Mark 9. Vigorously knead the dough again. On a floured work surface, roll out the dough to a thickness of about 2 cm/¾ inch, then place on the baking sheet and prick with a fork.

Cover with the onions and olives and sprinkle with garlic. Drizzle over the remaining oil, season with sea salt and crushed peppercorns and bake in the preheated oven for about 20 minutes.

Ciabatta

Ciabatta

First, make the biga. Sift the flour into a bowl, stir in the yeast and make a well in the centre. Pour in the water and stir until the dough comes together. Turn out onto a lightly floured work surface and knead for 5 minutes, until smooth and elastic. Shape the dough into a ball, put it into a bowl and put the bowl into a polythene bag or cover with a damp tea towel. Leave to rise in a warm place for 12 hours, until just beginning to collapse.

Gradually mix the water and milk into the biga, beating with a wooden spoon. Gradually mix in the flour and yeast with your hands, adding them a little at a time. Finally, mix in the salt and oil with your hands. The dough will be very wet; do not add extra flour. Put the bowl into a polythene bag or cover with a damp tea towel and leave the dough to rise in a warm place for 2 hours, until doubled in volume.

Dust 3 baking sheets with flour. Using a spatula, divide the dough between the prepared baking sheets without knocking out the air. With lightly floured hands, gently pull and shape each piece of dough into a rectangular loaf, then flatten slightly. Dust the tops of the loaves with flour and leave to rise in a warm place for 30 minutes.

Meanwhile, preheat the oven to 220°C/425°F/Gas Mark 7. Bake the loaves in the preheated oven for 25—30 minutes, until the crust is lightly golden and the loaves sound hollow when tapped on the base with your knuckles. Transfer to wire racks to cool.

We bring ciabatta
and salt whenever
we're invited to a
house-warming party!

makes 3 loaves

400 ml/14 fl oz lukewarm water
4 tbsp lukewarm lowfat milk
675 g/1 lb 8 oz strong white
    flour
1 sachet easy-blend dried yeast
2 tsp salt
3 tbsp olive oil

biga
450 g/1 lb strong white flour,
    plus extra for dusting
1¼ tsp easy-blend dried yeast
125 ml/4 fl oz lukewarm water

Mama's essential baking equipment

Some say that if cookery is an art, then baking is a science. Whereas with a stew or a sauce or a salad you can improvise and experiment, with baking you have to be strict. Stick to the measurements, follow the recipe carefully, or poof! Disastro! And that means that having the right equipment is vital.

One of the most common mistakes made when baking is forgetting the importance of allowing things to cool properly. I keep a stack of wire racks and have a space near the window for my baking to stand after it comes out of the oven. Not only does this allow the cooking process to finish properly, it fills the house and garden with the beautiful aroma of freshly baked bread!

My rolling pin belonged to my mama's mama. It's already promised to my Maria's daughter Fiorella. It's nothing to look at — but this long old wooden pin has helped three generations of women in my family feed their loved ones.

Measuring spoons and jugs should also be well-maintained. I keep two sets: one dry, one wet.

Lastly, a set of ice-cream scoops — in the old spring-loaded style — make scooping things into perfect balls so much easier than doing it by hand. Just remember to keep one aside for the gelato itself!

You need two kinds of spatula. A metal one with the thinnest edge you can find is a must, and I now use a rubber one too: it was a Christmas present from my great-grand-daughter Elena and I use it for folding.

Pane Joscano
Juscan unsalted bread

makes 1 large or 2 smaller loaves

500 g/1 lb 2 oz strong white
flour, plus extra for dusting
1½ tsp easy-blend dried yeast
2 tbsp olive oil, plus extra
for oiling
300 ml/10 fl oz lukewarm water

Mix the flour and yeast together in a mixing bowl.

Make a well in the centre. Mix the olive oil and water together in a jug and pour into the well. Gradually mix the liquid into the flour mixture with a round-bladed knife. Gather the mixture together with your hands to form a soft dough.

Turn out the dough onto a lightly floured work surface and knead for 5–7 minutes, or until very smooth and elastic. Return the dough to the bowl and cover with a clean tea towel or oiled clingfilm, then leave to rise in a warm place for 1 hour, or until doubled in size. Turn out and gently knead again for 1 minute, or until smooth.

Preheat the oven to 200°C/400°F/Gas Mark 6. Oil 1 or 2 baking sheets. Shape the dough into 1 large oval or 2 smaller ovals and transfer to the prepared sheet or sheets. Cover with a clean tea towel or oiled clingfilm and leave to rise in a warm place for 30 minutes.

Make several slashes in the top of the bread with a sharp knife. Bake in the preheated oven for 30–35 minutes (or 20–25 minutes for 2 loaves). If the bread is getting too brown, reduce the temperature a little. To test that the bread is cooked, turn it over and tap it on the base — it should sound hollow. Leave to cool on a wire rack.

Mama's Tip
The Tuscans like to eat salty, spicy food such as sausages. This traditional unsalted bread is an ideal accompaniment to their highly seasoned food.

Focaccia con cipolle e rosmarino
Flatbread with onion and rosemary

Mix the flour, yeast and salt together in a mixing bowl, then stir in the chopped rosemary. Make a well in the centre.

Mix 3 tablespoons of the oil with the water in a jug and pour into the well. Gradually mix the liquid into the flour mixture with a round-bladed knife. Gather the mixture together with your hands to form a soft dough.

Turn out the dough onto a lightly floured work surface and knead for 8—10 minutes, or until very smooth and elastic. Return the dough to the bowl and cover with a clean tea towel or oiled clingfilm, then leave to rise in a warm place for 45—60 minutes, or until doubled in size. Turn out and gently knead again for 1 minute, or until smooth. Preheat the oven to 200°C/400°F/ Gas Mark 6. Oil a baking sheet. Gently roll out the dough to a round about 30 cm/12 inches in diameter — it doesn't have to be a perfect circle; a slightly oval shape is traditional. Transfer to

Mama's Tip

Sun-dried tomatoes and chopped olives can be added before the final rising or just sprinkled on top for extra flavour.

makes 1 loaf

450 g/1 lb strong white flour,
    plus extra for dusting
1½ tsp easy-blend dried yeast
½ tsp salt
2 tbsp chopped fresh rosemary,
    plus extra small sprigs to
    garnish
5 tbsp extra virgin olive oil,
    plus extra for oiling
300 ml/10 fl oz lukewarm water
1 red onion, finely sliced and
    separated into rings
1 tbsp coarse sea salt,
    for sprinkling

the prepared sheet and cover with a clean tea towel or oiled clingfilm then leave to rise in a warm place for 20—30 minutes. Make holes about 5 cm/2 inches apart all over the surface of the dough with the handle of a wooden spoon. Spread the onion rings over the dough, then drizzle with the remaining oil and sprinkle over the sea salt. Bake in the preheated oven for 20—25 minutes, or until well risen and golden brown. Five minutes before the end of the cooking time, garnish with the rosemary sprigs. Transfer to a wire rack to cool for a few minutes, then serve the bread warm.

Pane con pesto ed olive
Pesto and olive soda bread

makes 1 loaf

350 g/12 oz plain flour
250 g/9 oz wholemeal flour
1 tsp bicarbonate of soda
½ tsp salt
3 tbsp pesto
300 ml/10 fl oz buttermilk
85 g/3 oz stoned green olives,
   coarsely chopped
olive oil, for greasing
milk, to glaze

Preheat the oven to 200°C/400°F/Gas Mark 6 and grease a baking sheet. Sift the flours, bicarbonate of soda and salt into a bowl, adding back any bran from the sieve.

Combine the pesto and buttermilk. Stir into the flour with the olives, mixing to a soft dough. Add more liquid if needed.

Shape the dough into a 20 cm/8 inch round and place on the baking sheet. Flatten slightly and cut a deep cross in the top with a sharp knife.

Brush with milk and bake for 30—35 minutes, until golden brown. The loaf should sound hollow when tapped on the base. Serve on the day of baking, with soup or cheese and salad for a healthy lunch.

Polenta Parmigiana
Parmesan polenta

serves 12

oil, for greasing
200 g/7 oz fine polenta
200 g/7 oz flour
4 tsp baking powder
2 tsp celery salt
85 g/3 oz grated Parmesan cheese
2 eggs, beaten
400 ml/14 fl oz milk
55 g/2 oz butter, melted
1 bunch spring onions, chopped
pepper

Preheat the oven to 190°C/375°F/Gas Mark 5. Grease a 23-cm/9-inch square baking tin.

Sift the polenta, flour, baking powder, celery salt and a pinch of pepper into a bowl and stir in 55 g/2 oz of the cheese.

Beat together the eggs, milk and melted butter.

Add the egg mixture to the dry ingredients and stir well to mix evenly.

Stir in the chopped spring onions and spread the mixture evenly into the prepared tin.

Sprinkle the remaining cheese over the mixture. Bake in the preheated oven for 30—35 minutes, or until firm and golden. Cut into squares and serve warm.

Parmesan Cheese

Torta di broccoli, pancetta e Gorgonzola
Broccoli, pancetta and Gorgonzola galette

serves 4

1 sheet ready-rolled frozen puff
  pastry, thawed
  (28 x 22 cm/11 x 8½ inches/
  half a 425-g/15-oz pack)
225 g/8 oz small broccoli
  florets, halved if necessary
100 g/3½ oz diced pancetta
1 small red onion, sliced
100 g/3½ oz Gorgonzola or
  other blue cheese, chopped
pepper
toasted pine kernels, to garnish

Preheat the oven to 200°C/400°C/Gas Mark 6.
Place the pastry on a baking sheet and lightly score a line
all around, cutting only halfway through, to within
1 cm/½ inch of the edge. Steam or boil the broccoli for
4–5 minutes, until just tender. Drain.

Fry the pancetta with the onion, stirring, until golden.
Stir in the broccoli and season with pepper. Spread
the broccoli mixture over the pastry, leaving the
border clear.

Scatter the pieces of cheese evenly over the top.
Bake the galette in the preheated oven for 25–30
minutes, until the pastry is risen and golden.

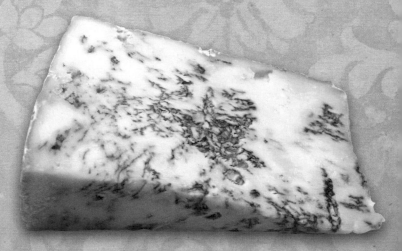

Gorgonzola Dolce

Mama's Tip
Sprinkle with
toasted pine kernels
and serve warm with
a tomato salad.

Caprino in crosta
Goat's cheese in pastry

serves 4

1 sachet easy-blend dried yeast
pinch of sugar
7 tbsp warm water
200 g/7 oz strong white flour,
   plus extra for dusting
½ tsp salt
2 tbsp olive oil, plus extra
   for greasing
1 tsp finely chopped fresh
   oregano
300 g/10½ oz fresh goat's cheese
   (log)
1 egg, separated

Dissolve the yeast and sugar in the warm water. Sift the flour into a bowl and make a well in the centre. Add the salt, oil and yeast–water mixture and knead everything into a smooth, silky dough. Form the dough into a ball, cover and set aside in a warm place for an hour, or until doubled in size.

Preheat the oven to 200°C/400°F/Gas Mark 6 and grease a baking sheet. Vigorously knead the dough once more, working in the oregano, then roll it out on a floured work surface.

Cut the cheese into 4 slices of equal thickness. Cut out 8 pastry rounds slightly larger than the cheese slices. Place a slice of cheese on 4 of the rounds and brush the edges of the dough with egg white. Cover with the remaining rounds and press the edges together firmly. Place the filled pockets on the baking sheet and brush with whisked egg yolk. Bake in the preheated oven for about 20 minutes.

Torta di pomodori e formaggio
Cheese and tomato tart

serves 4

125 g/4½ oz strong white flour
125 g/4½ oz self-raising flour
125 g/4½ oz chilled butter,
   diced
1 egg yolk
4 tbsp cold water
pinch of salt
oil, for greasing

filling
8-9 tomatoes, peeled, deseeded
   and cut into eighths
150 g/5½ oz coarsely grated
   Emmenthal cheese
4 eggs
100 ml/3½ fl oz double cream
2 tbsp chopped fresh oregano or
   marjoram
1 tbsp snipped fresh chives
pinch of salt

Sift the flours and salt into a bowl, then sift again. Work the butter into the flours, rubbing between your fingertips until the mixture resembles dry sand. Beat the egg yolk and water together and stir into the flour mixture with a fork. Once the dough starts to clump, knead very lightly to form a compact ball. Wrap in clingfilm and leave to chill in the refrigerator for at least 30 minutes.

Preheat the oven to 160°C/325°F/Gas Mark 3. Lightly grease a 28-cm/11-inch loose-based tart tin. Roll out the pastry very thinly and use to line the tin. Using the side of your forefinger, press the dough into the corner of the tin to raise it slightly above the rim. Line the pastry base with greaseproof paper and weigh down with dried beans. Bake blind in the preheated oven for 15 minutes.

Arrange the tomato segments in the pastry case in concentric circles. Sprinkle the grated cheese evenly over the top. Beat the eggs lightly, then stir in the cream, oregano, chives, and salt and pepper. Mix well, then pour into the pastry case. Return to the oven and bake for 20—25 minutes, until puffed and golden. Serve hot or warm.

Torta verde
Spinach pie

serves 6-8

250 g/9 oz plain flour,
  plus extra for dusting
5 tbsp olive oil, plus extra
  for greasing
1.5 kg/3 lb.5 oz leaf spinach
1 onion, finely chopped
1 garlic clove, finely chopped
5 eggs
100 g/3½ oz grated
  Parmesan cheese
1 egg yolk
salt and pepper

Sift the flour onto a work surface and make a well in the centre. Put 2 tablespoons of olive oil, a pinch of salt and 2—4 tablespoons of water into the well and knead everything into a smooth, supple dough.

Form the dough into a ball, cover it in clingfilm and leave to chill for 30 minutes in the refrigerator.

Bring a large saucepan of lightly salted water to the boil. Thoroughly wash the spinach, removing any wilted leaves and coarse stems. Plunge it into the boiling water and blanch it briefly. Pour off the hot water and refresh the spinach in cold water. Drain, then finely chop the spinach.

Preheat the oven to 200°C/400°F/Gas Mark 6 and grease a 25-cm/10-inch round springform cake tin.

Heat the remaining oil in a saucepan, add the onion and garlic and sauté briefly. Add the spinach, season with salt and pepper and sauté a few minutes longer, stirring constantly. Remove from the heat and leave to cool. Whisk the eggs, stir in the cheese, and combine with the spinach. Roll out the pastry on a floured work surface. Cut out two rounds of pastry the size of the base of the springform tin. Lay one round on the base of the tin and use scraps of pastry to form a border up the side. Spread the spinach mixture over the base, smoothing the surface, and lay the second pastry round on top.

Prick several holes in the top with a fork. Fold over the sides of the pastry and press together firmly. Decorate with the remaining pastry, if desired, and brush the surface with the egg yolk. Bake in the preheated oven for about 1 hour. Serve hot or cold.

Stromboli
Savoury roulade

makes 1 loaf

675 g/1 lb 8 oz strong white
    flour
2½ tsp easy-blend dried yeast
2 tsp sea salt flakes
3 tbsp olive oil, plus extra
    for greasing
350 ml/12 fl oz lukewarm water

filling
85 g/3 oz thinly sliced
    Italian salami
300 g/10½ oz diced mozzarella
    cheese
handful basil leaves
2 red peppers, roasted,
    peeled, deseeded and sliced
pepper

Combine the flour, yeast and 1½ teaspoons of the salt, then stir in the oil with enough water to make a soft dough.

Turn out the dough onto a floured work surface and knead for about 10 minutes. Cover and set aside in a warm place for 1 hour, until doubled in size.

Knead lightly for 2—3 minutes, until smooth. Cover and leave to stand for a further 10 minutes. Roll out the dough to a rectangle about 38 x 25 cm/15 x10 inches, and 1 cm/½ inch thick.

Preheat the oven to 220°C/425°F/Gas Mark 7. Grease a baking sheet. Spread the salami over the dough and top with the cheese, basil and red peppers. Season with pepper. Roll up firmly from the long side, pinch the ends and put on the prepared baking sheet. Join underneath, cover and leave to stand for 10 minutes.

Pierce the roll deeply several times with a skewer. Brush with oil and sprinkle with the remaining salt. Bake in the preheated oven for 30—35 minutes, or until firm and golden. Leave to cool on a wire rack. Serve fresh and warm, cut into thick slices.

Crostata di limone
Lemon tart

serves 6-8

200 g/7 oz plain flour
250 g/9 oz caster sugar,
    plus 2 tbsp
5 egg yolks
grated peel and juice of 2 lemons
1 pinch salt
100 g/3¼ oz chilled butter
3 eggs
150 ml/5 fl oz double cream
2 tbsp icing sugar
oil, for greasing

Sift the flour onto a work surface, blend in 7 tablespoons of the caster sugar, and make a well in the centre. Add 4 egg yolks, half the lemon peel, the salt and the butter, cut into small pieces. Knead everything into a smooth, supple dough. Form the dough into a ball, cover it in clingfilm and chill for 1 hour in the refrigerator.

Preheat the oven to 180°C/350°F/Gas Mark 4 and grease a 25-cm/10-inch round springform tart tin. Roll out the pastry very thinly on a floured work surface and use to line the base and sides of the tin. Use a fork to prick several holes in the pastry, then lay a sheet of baking paper over it. Fill with dried beans and bake for 15 minutes. Remove the dried beans and baking paper and leave the pastry case to cool.

Reduce the oven temperature to 160°C/325°F/Gas Mark 3. Beat the remaining egg yolk, the whole eggs and the rest of the sugar and lemon peel into a thick, pale cream. Stir in the lemon juice. Whip the cream and fold it into the egg mixture. Pour it into the case and spread evenly, then bake in the preheated oven for 20 minutes. Dust the surface with icing sugar, then return the tart to the oven until golden brown.

Brioche ai cioccolato e zafferano
Chocolate and saffron brioches

makes 12

pinch of saffron threads
3 tbsp boiling water
55 g/2 oz butter, melted
350 g/12 oz plain flour
pinch of salt
1 tbsp caster sugar
2½ tsp easy-blend dried yeast
2 eggs, beaten
6 squares plain chocolate,
    halved, 30 g/1 oz in total
milk, for glazing

Add the saffron to the boiling water and leave to cool completely.

Lightly brush 12 individual brioche tins or fluted patty tins with some of the butter.

Sift the flour, salt and sugar together and stir in the yeast. Add the saffron liquid, eggs and remaining butter to make a soft dough.

Knead until smooth, then cover and leave to stand in a warm place for 1—1½ hours, until doubled in size. Knead briefly, then shape three quarters of the dough into 12 balls. Place one in every tin and press a piece of chocolate firmly into each.

Shape the remaining dough into small balls with a pointed end. Brush with milk and press the balls into each brioche, sealing well.

Cover with oiled clingfilm and leave to stand in a warm place for 1½ hours, or until doubled in size. Meanwhile, preheat the oven to 200°C/400°F/Gas Mark 6. Brush the brioches with milk and bake in the preheated oven for 12—15 minutes, until firm and golden. Turn out and serve warm, for breakfast or with coffee.

Mama's tips for successful baking

A kitchen without fresh baking is like a house without laughter. You probably thought that baking your own ciabatta, focaccia, olive bread or pastry would be difficult, but Mama has shown you how easy it can be...

° As I said before, baking is more *scienza* than *arte*. Save self-expression for the finishing touches — for everything else, follow Mama to the letter. If the recipe calls for a 20-cm/8-inch tin, then an 18-cm/7-inch tin will not work!

° Remember why you're baking. Kitchens should not be a place for stress and worry. You're baking because you want to, because the smell and taste of fresh ciabatta are worth any difficulties in the recipe. Mama didn't get it right every time when she started either!

Mama's Tip

Don't be tempted to overbake. If anything, remove things from the oven a tad early, as the heat inside will keep them cooking even as they cool.

Always melt butter at low temperatures to avoid burning.

Don't be tempted to keep checking on your baking. Once things are in the oven, let them be. Opening the door lets out heat and will affect how things are cooked.

Mama's trick for measuring sticky stuff such as honey or melted chocolate: use the same jug as for measuring your oil. That way your honey will pour out without some of it sticking and getting left behind.

Remember — after the dough cleans the bowl and forms a ball on one side, do not add any more flour!

Biscotti ai mirtilli e pinoli
Cranberry and pine kernel biscotti

makes 18-20

100 g/3½ oz soft dark brown sugar
1 extra large egg
175 g/6 oz plain flour
½ tsp baking powder
1 tsp ground allspice
85 g/3 oz dried cranberries
55 g/2 oz pine kernels, toasted
butter or oil, for greasing

Preheat the oven to 180°C/350°F/Gas Mark 4. Grease a baking sheet.

Whisk the sugar with the egg until pale and thick enough to leave a trail when the whisk is lifted.

Sift the flour, baking powder and allspice into the bowl and fold into the mixture. Stir in the cranberries and pine kernels and mix lightly to a smooth dough.

With lightly floured hands, shape the mixture into a long roll, about 28 cm/11 inches long. Press to flatten slightly.

Lift the dough onto the prepared baking sheet and bake in the preheated oven for 20—25 minutes, until golden. Leave to cool for 3—4 minutes, then cut into 15 mm/5⁄8 inch thick slices and arrange flat on the baking sheet.

Bake the slices for about 10 minutes, until golden. Leave to cool on a wire rack. When cool, store the biscotti in an airtight container for 2—3 weeks.

Biscotti con arancia ed amarena
Orange and sour cherry biscotti

makes 20-30

150 g/5½ oz whole blanched
  almonds
100 g/3½ oz dried sour cherries
  or dried cranberries
100 g/3½ oz pine kernels
140 g/5oz plain flour, plus
  extra for dusting
175 g/6 oz caster sugar
1 tsp baking powder
¼ tsp ground nutmeg
¼ tsp ground cinnamon
zest of 1 orange
2 eggs
2 tsp vanilla extract

Preheat the oven to 180°C/350°F/Gas Mark 4. Line two baking sheets with parchment paper. Roughly chop the almonds and the cherries. Place in a bowl with the whole pine kernels. Mix the flour, sugar, baking powder, nutmeg, cinnamon and orange zest with the nuts and dried fruit.

Beat the eggs and the vanilla extract together. When combined, add the flour mixture and combine to form a firm dough. Turn out the dough onto a lightly floured work surface. Knead for 4—5 minutes, or until no longer sticky. Divide the dough in two, and shape each piece into a long flat log, about 5 cm/2 inches wide. Transfer the logs to the prepared baking sheets. Place in the preheated oven and bake for 20—25 minutes, until pale golden brown in colour.

Remove from the oven and leave to cool for 5 minutes. Reduce the oven temperature to 160°C/325°F/Gas Mark 3. Transfer the baked loaves to a chopping board and, using a serrated knife, cut into 1-cm/½-inch slices. Arrange the slices flat on the lined baking sheets and return to the oven. Bake for about 15—20 minutes, until dry and crisp. Remove from the oven and leave to cool. Store in an airtight container.

Torta di mandorle
Almond cake

Preheat the oven to 160°C/325°F/Gas Mark 3. Generously grease a 20-cm/8-inch round springform cake tin. Beat the egg yolks with the caster sugar in a medium-sized bowl until pale and thick and the mixture leaves a ribbon trail when the whisk is lifted. Stir in the flour, almonds, orange rind and orange juice.

Whisk the egg whites with a pinch of salt in another bowl until stiff. Gently fold the whites into the egg yolk mixture.

Pour the mixture into the prepared tin and bake in the preheated oven for 50—60 minutes, until golden and just firm to the touch. Turn out onto a wire rack to cool. Sift over a little icing sugar to decorate before serving.

Makes 12-14

butter, for greasing
3 eggs, separated
200 g/7 oz caster sugar
70 g/2½ oz potato flour
115 g/4 oz almonds, blanched, peeled and finely chopped
finely grated rind of 1 orange
125 ml/4 fl oz orange juice
pinch of salt
icing sugar, for dusting

Fiorentini
Florentines

Preheat the oven to 180°C/350°F/Gas Mark 4. Grease and flour 2 baking sheets or line with baking paper.

Place the butter in a small saucepan and heat gently until melted. Add the sugar, stir until dissolved, then bring the mixture to the boil. Remove from the heat and stir in the sultanas, cherries, ginger, sunflower seeds and almonds. Mix well, then beat in the cream.

Place small teaspoons of the fruit and nut mixture on the prepared baking sheets, allowing plenty of space for the mixture to spread. Bake in the preheated oven for 10—12 minutes, or until light golden in colour.

Remove from the oven and, while still hot, use a round biscuit cutter to pull in the edges to form a perfect circle. Leave to cool and crisp before removing from the baking sheets.

Melt three-quarters of the chocolate and spread it on a sheet of baking paper. When the chocolate is on the point of setting, place the florentines flat-side down on the chocolate and allow to harden completely.

Cut around the florentines and remove from the baking paper. Spread a little more chocolate on the coated side of the florentines and use a fork to mark waves in the chocolate. Leave to set. Arrange on a plate with alternate sides facing upwards. Keep cool.

makes about 40

75 g/2¾ oz butter, plus extra
    for greasing
60 g/2¼ oz caster sugar
2 tbsp sultanas or raisins
2 tbsp glacé cherries, chopped
2 tbsp stem ginger, chopped
25 g/1 oz sunflower seeds
100 g/3½ oz flaked almonds
2 tbsp double cream
175 g/6 oz plain chocolate
flour, for dusting

Acknowledgements

The publisher would like to thank the following for permission to reproduce copyright material:

© Corbis:

8 (bottom, left) Little girl wearing dress

9 (bottom, right) Italian delicatessen storefront

12 (middle, right) Illustration of child dressed in bird of paradise costume

27 (bottom, right) The Common Cock Illustration

58 (middle, left) Young girl holding birthday cake

92 (middle, top) Girl hiding under mother's dress

134 (bottom, right) Illustration of child dressed in sparrow costume

134 (middle, left) Two children sitting in surf on beach

142 (middle, left) Father and son share watermelon at picnic

169 (middle, right) Adults carrying children on shoulders

176 (top, left) Baking cookies

177 (bottom, right) Many Happy Returns of the Day postcard with St. Bernard

180 (top, left) Red onion layers

180 (bottom, left) Shallots

190 (bottom, left) Illustration of a couple in a canoe

© Getty:

11 (bottom, middle) Basil leaves on white background

Front cover, Dried pasta, close-up

Front cover, 92 Various forms of pasta

127 (middle, left) Girl (4-5) having breakfast, (B&W)

143 (bottom, left) Family eating outdoors

© Sabine Vonderstein:

10 (bottom, left) Genova book

26 (left), 102 (left) striped ribbon

36 (left), 43 (right) 96 (left) green spot ribbon

52 (top, left), 58 (top, right) Postcard with girl

86—87, 128—129 (left, right), pink spot ribbon

100—101 Numbers x 10

135 (top, right) Brooch

© istockphoto.com:

All other incidental images not listed above

© Parragon Books Ltd:

All recipe images

Index

almonds
  almond biscuits 170–171
  almond cake 214
  figs with Gorgonzola 150
  orange and sour cherry biscotti 212
  Tuscan Christmas cake 90
  white tiramisù with strawberries 86
anchovies
  crostini with olive paste 162
  deep-fried mozzarella 104
apricots
  apricot ice cream 50
  Tuscan Christmas cake 90
artichokes
  artichokes with seafood 80
  four seasons pizza 95
  seared tuna with white beans and
    artichokes 42–43
asparagus
  asparagus and prosciutto
    wraps 148
  risotto with asparagus 54
  stuffed chicken breasts 74
aubergines
  country-style marinated aubergine
    slices 60
  mixed vegetables in oil 138

bacon and pancetta
  beef lasagne with ricotta and
    mozzarella 120–121
  Bolognese sauce 116
  broccoli, pancetta, and Gorgonzola
    galette 194–195
  chicken cacciatore 72
  mushrooms stuffed with bacon and
    spinach 34–35
  rice and peas 166–167
  spaghetti carbonara 118
beef
  beef braised in red wine 68–69
  beef lasagne with ricotta and
    mozzarella 120–121
  beef roulades with pecorino 66
  Bolognese sauce 116
  spaghetti with meatballs 38
borlotti beans

minestrone 14
  Tuscan bean soup 18
bread
  bread and tomato soup 16
  bruschetta with mozzarella 154
  cheese and sun-dried tomato
    toasts 156
  ciabatta 182–183
  deep-fried mozzarella 104
  flatbread with onion and
    rosemary 188–189
  flatbread with onions 180
  ham and rocket sandwiches 146
  homemade olive bread 178
  panettone bread-and-butter
    pudding 130
  pesto and olive soda bread 190
  prawn sandwiches 147
  savoury roulade 202
  tuna sandwiches 147
  Tuscan unsalted bread 186–187
  wild mushroom bruschetta 32
  see also crostini
broad bean and pecorino salad 152
broccoli, pancetta, and Gorgonzola
    galette 194–195

cannellini beans
  green and white bean salad 22
  seared tuna with white beans and
    artichokes 42–43
  Tuscan bean soup 18
cheese
  artichokes with seafood 80
  asparagus and prosciutto
    wraps 148
  beef lasagne with ricotta and
    mozzarella 120–121
  beef roulades with pecorino 66
  broad bean and pecorino salad 152
  broccoli, pancetta, and Gorgonzola
    galette 194–195
  bruschetta with mozzarella 154
  cheese and sun-dried tomato
    toasts 156
  cheese and tomato tart 198
  crostini with tomatoes 163

deep-fried mozzarella 104
  farfalle with sun-dried
    tomatoes 110
  figs with Gorgonzola 150
  four seasons pizza 95
  fried cheese pastries 158
  goat's cheese in pastry 196
  mariner's pizza 94
  Parmesan polenta 192
  pizza Margherita 95
  polenta with fontina 62
  pumpkin ravioli 108
  ravioli with feta cheese 109
  Roman-style gnocchi 114
  savoury roulade 202
  seafood omelette 36
  spaghetti carbonara 118
  spinach cannelloni 112
  spinach and mozzarella
    omelette 98
  spinach pie 200–201
  spinach and ricotta patties 102
  stuffed chicken breasts 74
  tiramisù 132
  white tiramisù with strawberries 86
cherries
  florentines 216–217
  orange and sour cherry biscotti 212
chicken
  braised chicken salad 26–27
  chicken cacciatore 72
  chicken morsels fried in batter 40
  crostini with chicken liver pâté 162
  stuffed chicken breasts 74
chocolate
  chocolate and saffron brioches 206
  florentines 216–217
  soft chocolate cake 172
  tiramisù 132
  white tiramisù with strawberries 86
ciabatta 182–183
courgettes
  mixed vegetables in oil 138
  seafood omelette 36
cranberry and pine kernel biscotti 210
crostini
  crostini with chicken liver pâté 162

crostini with herbs and
    tomatoes 162
  crostini with olive paste 162
  crostini with tomatoes 163

duck with vegetables 76

eggs
  cheese and tomato tart 198
  deep-fried mozzarella 104
  frittata with parsley 96
  lemon tart 204
  panettone bread-and-butter
    pudding 130
  prawn sandwiches 147
  soft chocolate cake 172
  spaghetti carbonara 118
  spinach and mozzarella
    omelette 98
  spinach pie 200–201
  tiramisù 132
  tuna sandwiches 147
  tuna-stuffed tomatoes 144
  zabaglione 128

fennel
  Livorno seafood stew 124–125
  potato and fennel bake 106–107
figs
  figs with Gorgonzola 150
  fruit salad 49
  ham and salami salad with figs 28
  mixed antipasti meat platter 30
fish and seafood
  artichokes with seafood 80
  baked scallops 44
  lightly battered and fried fish 122
  Livorno seafood stew 124–125
  marinated clams 78
  see also anchovies; prawns; squid;
tuna
florentines 216–17
French beans
  green and white bean salad 22
  seafood omelette 36

gnocchi: Roman-style gnocchi 114

ham
    beef roulades with pecorino 66
    four seasons pizza 95
    fried cheese pastries 158
    ham and rocket sandwiches 146
    see also prosciutto

lemons
    artichokes with seafood 80
    lemon tart 204
    Milanese-style osso buco 64
    olives with orange and lemon 140

Mama's tips
    big meal equipment 84–85
    "big Italian" gathering 58–59
    entertaining the children 168–169
    essential baking equipment 184–185
    essential picnic equipment 142–143
    feeding a big family 46–47
    running a smooth household 20–21
    staying cheerful 100–101
    successful baking 208–209
    taking it easy 126–127
minestrone 14
mushrooms
    Bolognese sauce 116
    four seasons pizza 95
    mixed vegetables in oil 138
    mushrooms preserved in oil 136
    mushrooms stuffed with bacon and
        spinach 34–35
    risotto with ceps 57
    seafood omelette 36
    wild mushroom bruschetta 32

olives
    beef roulades with pecorino 66
    crostini with olive paste 162
    deep-fried mozzarella 104
    flatbread with onions 180
    four seasons pizza 95
    green and white bean salad 22
    homemade olive bread 178
    mariner's pizza 94
    mixed antipasto meat platter 30
    olives with orange and lemon 140

pesto and olive soda bread 190
    seared tuna with white beans and
        artichokes 42–43
oranges
    almond cake 214
    deep-fried pastry ribbons 174
    fruit salad 49
    olives with orange and lemon 140
    orange and sour cherry biscotti 212
    Tuscan Christmas cake 90

panettone bread-and-butter
        pudding 130
panna cotta 48
pasta
    beef lasagne with ricotta and
        mozzarella 120–121
    farfalle with sun-dried
        tomatoes 110
    minestrone 14
    pumpkin ravioli 108
    ravioli with feta cheese 109
    spaghetti carbonara 118
    spaghetti with meatballs 38
    spinach cannelloni 112
    Tuscan bean soup 18
pears
    fruit salad 49
    poached pears in Marsala 88–89
peas
    minestrone 14
    rice and peas 166–167
peppers
    minestrone 14
    savoury roulade 202
    spinach and mozzarella omelette 98
pesto
    asparagus and prosciutto
        wraps 148
    pesto and olive soda bread 190
pizzas
    basic pizza dough 94
    four seasons pizza 95
    mariner's pizza 94
    pizza Margherita 95
polenta
    Parmesan polenta 192

polenta with fontina 62
pork stew 70
potato and fennel bake 106–107
prawns
    lightly battered and fried fish 122
    Livorno seafood stew 124–125
    pan-fried prawns 82
    prawn sandwiches 147
    seafood omelette 36
prosciutto
    asparagus and prosciutto
        wraps 148
    ham and salami salad with figs 28
    minestrone 14
    mixed antipasto meat platter 30
    prosciutto with rocket 164
    risotto with ceps 57
    stuffed chicken breasts 74
pumpkin ravioli 108

rice
    rice and peas 166–167
    see also risotto
risotto
    black risotto with squid 56
    risotto with asparagus 54
    risotto with ceps 57
rocket
    broad bean and pecorino salad 152
    ham and rocket sandwiches 146
    ham and salami salad with figs 28
    prosciutto with rocket 164

salami
    fried cheese pastries 158
    ham and salami salad with figs 28
    mixed antipasto meat platter 30
    savoury roulade 202
sausage
    beef lasagne with ricotta and
        mozzarella 120–121
    mixed antipasto meat platter 30
spinach
    mushrooms stuffed with bacon and
        spinach 34–35
    spinach and mozzarella omelette 98
    spinach pie 200–201

spinach and ricotta patties 102
squid
    black risotto with squid 56
    lightly battered and fried fish 122
    Livorno seafood stew 124–125
strawberries
    panna cotta 48
    white tiramisù with strawberries 86

tiramisù 132
tomatoes
    Bolognese sauce 116
    bread and tomato soup 16
    bruschetta with mozzarella 154
    cheese and sun-dried tomato
        toasts 156
    cheese and tomato tart 198
    chicken cacciatore 72
    country-style marinated aubergine
        slices 60
    crostini with herbs and
        tomatoes 162
    crostini with tomatoes 163
    farfalle with sun-dried
        tomatoes 110
    four seasons pizza 95
    Livorno seafood stew 124–125
    mariner's pizza 94
    Milanese-style osso buco 64
    minestrone 14
    mixed antipasto meat platter 30
    pizza Margherita 95
    pork stew 70
    seared tuna with white beans and
        artichokes 42–43
    spaghetti with meatballs 38
    tomato salad with cucumber 24
    tomato tart 160–161
    tuna-stuffed tomatoes 144
tuna
    seafood omelette 36
    seared tuna with white beans and
        artichokes 42–43
    tuna-stuffed tomatoes 144

veal: Milanese-style osso buco 64

zabaglione 128